'Margie Warrell has done it again! Just when we might be feeling in need of encouraging words and advice, she's back with a book that challenges each of us to draw from within, to lend a hand to others and to reach higher without fear. Do yourself a favour and read it soon.'

—**Kathy Calvin**, President & CEO,
United Nations Foundation

'*Make Your Mark* provides a roadmap to move past the fears and over the hurdles holding you back so you can create a life that lights you up. Read. Now.'

—**Estelle**, Grammy award winning singer-songwriter

'Written by a true master, *Make Your Mark* is your step-by-step guide to a life filled with passion and purpose. Highly practical, filled with wisdom and inspiration, this is a must read for anyone who wants to live a bigger life.'

—**Louisa Jewell**, President, Canadian Positive
Psychology Association

'If you've got big dreams but self-doubt keeps you from going after them, then this book has found its way to your hands for a reason. It's pointing you toward your biggest life. Read. Dare. Do.'

—**Jacqui Cooper**, Olympic Aerial Skier

'I'm a big fan of Margie Warrell for both her practical uplifting work and what it draws out in me and all her readers. As with her other books, *Make Your Mark* provides clear guidance, practical tools, and deep wisdom, all focused on one aim: inspiring a better you. Read this book and you'll truly Make Your Mark!"

—**Bill Treasurer**, Author of *Courage Goes to Work* and
Leaders Open Doors

'*Make Your Mark* will show you how to develop the habits and mindset to take control of your destiny and create a life of impact and purpose.'

—**Richard Reirson**, Leadership Consultant

T0052624

'If you've ever asked yourself "What if?" or "What more?" this is the book for you. *Make Your Mark* is the ultimate guide to fearlessly creating the life of your dreams.'
— **Janine Garner**, Author of *From Me To We*

'Never doubt the mark you can make when you commit to a purpose bigger than yourself. This book will show you how.'
— **Jacinta McDonell**, Co-founder, Anytime Fitness Australia & Founder, Human Kind Project and Urban Yoga

'Margie Warrell has done it again … this book shows what's holding you back while igniting the spark of courage to light your path forward. Part wisdom guide, part workbook, *Make Your Mark* is the best gift you can give yourself or someone you love.'
— **Suzi Pomerantz**, CEO, Innovative Leadership International

'*Make Your Mark* is a must read for anyone who isn't ready to settle for less than the biggest life they are capable of living. Buy it. Read it. Live it.'
— **Michelle McQuaid**, Author of *Lead Like A Woman*

MARGIE WARRELL

A GUIDEBOOK FOR THE
BRAVE HEARTED

WILEY

First published in 2017 by John Wiley & Sons Australia, Ltd
42 McDougall St, Milton Qld 4064
Office also in Melbourne

Typeset in 8.75/12.25 pt Caecilia LT Std

© Margie Warrell Global Pty Ltd 2017

The moral rights of the author have been asserted

National Library of Australia Cataloguing-in-Publication data:

Author:	Warrell, Margie, author
Title:	Make Your Mark: A Guidebook for the Brave Hearted / Margie Warrell
ISBN:	9780730343233 (pbk.)
	9780730343240 (ebook)
Subjects:	Self-actualization (Psychology).
	Self-confidence.
	Conduct of Life.
	Success.

Cover design: Delia Sala / Wiley

Cover images: © Undrey/Shutterstock; © solarbird/Shutterstock; © Angie Makes/Shutterstock; © TabitaZn/Shutterstock

Author photo: Alise Black

Printed in Singapore by C.O.S. Printers Pte Ltd

10 9 8 7 6 5 4 3 2

Disclaimer

The material in this publication is of the nature of general comment only, and does not represent professional advice. It is not intended to provide specific guidance for particular circumstances and it should not be relied on as the basis for any decision to take action or not take action on any matter which it covers. Readers should obtain professional advice where appropriate, before making any such decision. To the maximum extent permitted by law, the author and publisher disclaim all responsibility and liability to any person, arising directly or indirectly from any person taking or not taking action based on the information in this publication.

CONTENTS

STEP 4

EXIT THE SAFE LANE   83

Growth and comfort can't travel the same path

STEP 5

LEAN INTO THE CURVES   129

Life doesn't happen to you, it happens for you

STEP 6

BUILD YOUR TRIBE   157

We're braver together than we can ever be alone

STEP 7

RUN YOUR OWN BEST RACE 183

Bring your best self to your biggest challenges

ABOUT THE AUTHOR

Find Your Courage, Stop Playing Safe, Brave.

The titles of Margie's three previous bestselling books reflect her passion for helping people make braver decisions and lead bigger lives.

Margie's had to find her courage many times since growing up as the big sister of seven on a dairy farm in rural Australia. Personal struggles, family tragedies, an armed robbery, having four children in five years: all have taught her valuable lessons about embracing change, building resilience and the power of purpose.

Today Margie draws on her background in Fortune 500 business, coaching and psychology to equip people with the mindset and strategies needed to achieve stronger outcomes for themselves and others. Her clients include NASA, Accenture, Johnson & Johnson, Facebook, Mars, Australian Federal Police, Microsoft, Oracle, and the United Nations Foundation.

Host of RawCourage.TV, Margie's insights have also been shaped by her work and interviews with leaders and luminaries such as Sir Richard Branson, Bill Marriott and Marianne Williamson. Margie has also co-authored two other books with world leadership experts Stephen Covey, Jack Canfield, Ken Blanchard and John Gray.

An acclaimed keynote speaker and guest lecturer at Columbia and Georgetown universities, Margie is a sought-after commentator with leading media including *The Wall Street Journal*, Fox News, the *Today* show, Al Jazeera, *Women's Health* and *Inc. Magazine*. Her Forbes 'Courage Works' column has been read by millions.

A passionate advocate for gender equality, in 2010 Margie founded Global Courage to help women be stronger leaders across all sectors of society. She has since been appointed Australia's first Ambassador for Women in Global Business and has been made a Women's Economic Forum honouree. Margie is also an ambassador for Beyond Blue, and is committed to helping remove the stigma around mental illness and reducing the suffering of all those affected by it.

An adventurer at heart, Margie has travelled off the beaten track in 70-plus countries. She's crossed the Sahara desert, stayed in Palestinian refugee camps, swum with piranhas in the Amazon, cycled the streets of Beijing, hiked the Inca trail, coached women in Africa's infamous Kibera slum and spent three years living in Papua New Guinea.

When she's not juggling (and occasionally dropping) the many balls of making her own mark upon the world while raising her four teenage children (her proudest achievement), she enjoys planning adventures with them and her husband Andrew—most recently, summiting Mt Kilimanjaro.

For inspiration and information please visit www.margiewarrell.com.

ACKNOWLEDGEMENTS

An agent recently asked me if I had a five-year strategic plan for writing books. I told her it sounded like a great idea but, no, I didn't. This book, like all my others, evolved very organically from a casual conversation with my publisher, Lucy Raymond, about how I might self-publish a journal-style guidebook to share with clients and people at my workshops and Live Brave events. The original vision was largely just questions, a few quotes, empty pages and little else. As you can see, it has turned into something far bigger. So thank you, Lucy, for believing in me—a third time around—and allowing the scope and structure of this book to evolve as I dived into writing it. Thanks also to the team at Wiley who helped shepherd it into your hands right now.

Given this is my fourth book, it would be reasonable to assume I'd have this whole 'book-birthing' process down to a fine art by now. Aaagh ... if only that were true! From starting my first book *Find Your Courage*—when I had four kids under the age of seven (probably more crazy than courageous)—to this one, bringing a book to life while keeping up with my own has always been a juggling act. Disappearing for three months to a quiet cabin in the woods has simply not been an option. So, of all the people deserving of acknowledgement, my husband Andrew tops the list. Sharing my life with someone who is also my biggest cheerleader is a blessing I count daily. Or *most* days ... some I forget.

I also want to acknowledge the many big-hearted people who make up my 'tribe'. My friends, whom I can always count on to make me laugh, let me cry and to have the occasional vent with when my best-laid plans fall apart (which happened while writing this book ... but I'll save that for another day). In particular, to Anna Quin, Christine Louden, Emma Hogan, Sarah Garrow ... thank you for your listening ear and loving support at crucial moments throughout the last year as this book came into being. Also to my treasured family—Mum, Dad, Cath, Anne, Steve, Pauline and Frank—and co.! I'm so blessed to be part of the Kleinitz clan.

A shout-out also to my team—Val, Kim, James and Angela—for having my back and supporting me as I work to make my own mark. Also to Sal Bonney, Margie Edmonds and my generous in-laws, Chris and Di Warrell, for helping on the home front. It takes a village and I'm so glad you're in mine!

Finally, I want to acknowledge my four genuinely remarkable teenage children—Lachlan, Maddy, Ben and Matthew—who make me look like a good mum despite my shortfalls. Your advice on how to be a better parent, use hashtags, upgrade my 80s dance moves, sneeze more quietly and 'get my act together' is both highly grounding and indispensable. While I know you feel you have enough books to read at school without one more added to the list, I hope that when you do finally pick this one up you'll find some small piece of advice you haven't heard already. You each have a uniquely important mark to make on this world, and encouraging you to make it is my greatest privilege.

—*Margie*

INTRODUCTION

I'm truly grateful this book has found its way into your hands.

I wrote it for you because I know you have a heartfelt desire to live a deeply meaningful life, one that inspires you even as it challenges you. A life rich in purpose and fused with passion. A life you can one day look back upon without regret but with a deep sense of satisfaction, gratitude and wonder.

Yet I am guessing that there are times you find yourself feeling stuck, wondering whether there is more to life than the one you are living. Whether there is more you could be doing. Whether you are playing too small, living too safe or settling for too little.

I've felt that way myself. Many times. Sometimes I still do. Times when my desire to stamp my biggest mark upon the world is wrestled to the ground by my fear that I simply don't have what it takes; that I'm deluding myself and I'm destined to fall short of the mark. Far short.

Which is what has brought us together, here, right now. Because I know that I'm not alone: that there are millions like me who also sometimes wonder, 'What else?' or 'What if?' People with wonderful talents and burning dreams who want to do more and be more, but who so often doubt whether they can. People like you and me who aren't content to settle for less than the life we are capable of living, but who so easily get swept along by the shallow currents of our culture. A culture that celebrates the superficial which feeds our ego, at the expense of the meaningful which feeds our soul.

Of course, there is no shortage of social-media posts and t-shirts emblazoned with catchphrases imploring us to *Think Big*, *Shoot for the Stars* and *#JustDoIt*.

Few people would argue with their sentiments.

After all, to quote one of the most well-worn maxims, 'life is not a dress rehearsal', right?

Yet, for all the messages we get encouraging us to 'lean in' and 'aim high', most people struggle to live them out. This is despite the thousands of books written to help them do just that. (I've written three myself.) While most of these books offer useful insights to help move people into action, they often fall short in transforming the lives of their readers or of their families, teams, organisations and communities.

The reason is simple.

FORGING A DEEPLY MEANINGFUL LIFE IS FRAUGHT WITH RISK.

The risk of failure, the risk of rejection, falling flat on your face and feeling like a fool.

Given we're wired to avoid all these risks, it's little wonder so many people veer away from them. Taking the road less travelled just seems so hard.

Too hard.

It's hard because, at the core of our being and woven through every thread of our psychological DNA, we are terrified of falling short—far short—of achieving our goals, much less 'reaching the stars' or leaving a legacy that will far outlast our years on earth.

Hardwired into our boards at birth is a potent and primal force against change: against exposing ourselves to anything that might threaten our sense of identity, security and belonging.

AND SO, FOR ALL OUR GOOD INTENTIONS TO BE STRONG AND BRAVE, WE SO OFTEN HOLD BACK FROM DOING THE VERY THINGS WE KNOW DEEP IN OUR HEARTS WILL HELP US CREATE MORE OF WHAT WE WANT AND TO CHANGE WHAT WE DON'T.

More fulfilment, more connection, more growth.

Less melancholy, less conflict, less spinning our wheels in a frenzy of busyness without feeling like we're moving any closer towards the very things we yearn for most.

Hence this book.

Since embarking upon my 'second career' nearly 20 years ago, I've had the privilege of working with thousands of people from different walks of life and cultures around the world. Entrepreneurs. Small-business owners. Leaders in business, government, education, healthcare and social enterprise. Time and time again, what I have found is that while they often come to me looking for answers, the most powerful answers they ever get are those they arrive at themselves when they sit quietly, unguardedly, with the big questions.

What is your ultimate outcome? What do you yearn for most, when all that sparkles is stripped away? Where is fear holding the balance of power in your life? Is the security it's giving you worth what you're giving up? What would be possible if you stepped outside your story?

These are just a few of the questions I've asked people over the years to help them on their 'quest' to live a deeply authentic and meaningful life. I share them here only because I know that if you sit quietly with these questions you'll find yourself having to think a little harder and dig a little deeper about your own.

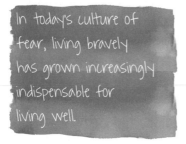

In today's culture of fear, living bravely has grown increasingly indispensable for living well.

With both my clients and the people who have attended my programs, I have witnessed the power that flows when we give ourselves the emotional space to connect to our deepest desires and uncover the fears holding them hostage. The possibilities that can open up when we remove our armour and get clear about the highest purpose for our lives—the most meaningful mark we hope to make on the world—are as boundless as they are beautiful.

It's why this book is different from others I've written or the many wonderful books that may already line your shelves. While it's far more than a journal, my intention for writing it is to help you access the wisdom already inside you, uncovering your own answers to life's most pressing questions.

As such, I have deliberately excluded anything I felt could distract from or dilute the impact of the questions. While all of the concepts in the book are backed by empirical research, it doesn't detail studies about the psychology of risk-taking, the neuroscience of peak performance or the importance of cultivating grit and a 'growth mindset'. Nor does it contain the case studies I've included in my previous books. All these have their place, and it's an important one. It just isn't here.

My primary goal for this book is to guide you on a journey to chart your bravest course to your biggest life. To do that, you'll need to be really honest about what you most want and what's kept you from having it already—or having *more* of it!

That in itself will take courage. To pause from the busyness of your doing and to spend more time simply being. To step beyond the shallows and dive deep into the still waters so seldom entered. To embrace your vulnerability and interrogate your reality. To park your cynicism, confront your fears and see yourself as a leader with an invaluable mark to make—both on the people you care about most and those you may never get to meet.

BUT LET'S FACE IT, WE HUMANS ARE WIZARDS WHEN IT COMES TO DISTRACTING OURSELVES FROM THE REAL WORK OF THINKING HARD ABOUT LIVING WELL.

We hurry through our days, from one activity to the next, juggling balls, spinning plates and bending ourselves inside out to measure up or avoid missing out. All the while we never quite get around to getting real about our inner lives or, to quote industrialist John W Gardner, 'to probe the fearful and wonderful world within'.

It's my hope that this book will help you to probe the 'fearful and wonderful world within' so that you can avoid the barrenness of a busy life and relish the richness of a brave one.

I must warn you, though. The journey ahead won't always be comfortable. Then again, having spent so much of my adult life feeling decidedly uncomfortable, I know that no worthwhile endeavour ever is.

WHAT I'VE LEARNED SINCE GROWING UP ON A FARM WITH A VISION THAT EXTENDED LITTLE BEYOND THE BACK PADDOCK, IS THAT OUR LIVES ARE AS BIG AS WE DARE TO MAKE THEM.

It's why you cannot afford to wait until 'one day' before you make time to create the highest vision for your life. *One day*, when your kids are older. *One day*, when the economy's better. *One day*, when the mortgage is paid. *One day*, when you've lost your doubt or 'found yourself' and finally feel like you've grown up.

There is no 'one day'. There is only 'this day'. Today.

While you may be tempted to skirt over the questions that follow each chapter and the exercises at the end of each of the seven steps—which tie the whole book together—I can't overstate the value you'll get from actually writing down your answers. Research has proven that the very process of putting a pen to paper will help you to process your emotions and refine your thinking in ways that simply reading never will.

Truly.

That said, there is no right or wrong way to complete this book. While it comprises seven distinct steps that guide you through a journey from self-reflection to purposeful action, if you open any page, you will find an invitation to rethink how you're 'doing life'.

As I wrote in *Brave* (a book that provides a valuable companion to this one), if it were easy to lay our vulnerability on the line for something more important—to risk what we have now for what we want most—we would all be doing it. It's why, in our increasingly uptight, cautious and uncertain world, living your best life requires living a brave life.

I hope this book will serve as a roadmap—your own personal 'life GPS'—to help you navigate from where you are now to where you most want to go (and, if you're unsure where that is, to help you figure it out!). So as you write down your thoughts, reframe your fears and reimagine your future in the pages to come, I invite you to do so with a brave heart and open mind.

YOUR FUTURE IS STILL AN OPEN BOOK, WAITING TO BE WRITTEN. YOU ARE ITS AUTHOR.

Every step of your journey so far has held a gift for you to use to start a new chapter. But not just any chapter. One that casts you as the hero in this grand adventure of life and leaves an indelible mark on others for how you lived it.

No-one on earth has the same combination of know-how, talent, passion, personality, opportunity or hard-won wisdom as you. No-one ever will. If this book helps you channel the best of who you are into making the biggest mark you can, I will be deeply honoured and immeasurably grateful.

Thank you for trusting me to accompany you on this leg of your journey.

In return I ask just one thing: to trust in yourself that you have everything—and I mean *everything*—you need within you to fulfil the highest vision you are inspired to pursue.

You were born with wings, why prefer to crawl through life?

RUMI

DECIDE WHAT YOU STAND FOR

YOU ARE HERE TO MAKE A MARK
THAT NO-ONE ELSE CAN. OWN
YOUR DIFFERENCE. RE-IMAGINE
YOUR FUTURE. STAND FOR A CAUSE
FAR GREATER THAN YOURSELF.

We all have different ideas of how to be happy. Some work—sort of, or at least part of the time. Others don't. In fact, sometimes people can make themselves royally miserable in their misguided quest for happiness. (They can make life tough going for others too!)

We humans are complex creatures with a vast host of needs and desires, biases and beliefs, often wrestling with each other behind the mask we wear for the world. Some of them we can articulate; others we can't. But they are there nevertheless, in the background, out of sight—often even out of our conscious awareness—guiding our choices, directing our actions and steering us away from anything that might be perceived as remotely threatening to our safety or sense of identity. It's why, despite the pickle some people can get themselves into they continue to do more of what's already not working in the naïve, if not deluded, hope that eventually it will.

The reason is simple: whatever we're doing, it is always meeting a need on some level. A need for belonging, approval or admiration. A need for security, safety or certainty. A need for prestige and power. A need for pity, to prove our unworthiness or to validate our powerlessness.

ON SOME LEVEL, EVERY DECISION WE MAKE PROVIDES A PSYCHOLOGICAL PAY-OFF, EVEN IF THAT PAY-OFF IS CAUSING US ALL SORTS OF GRIEF AND ONLY PERPETUATING THE PROBLEMS WE COMPLAIN ABOUT.

Of course, that's not to say we don't have other higher level needs and desires—for growth, for giving, for exploring, for expressing ourselves fully in the world and leaving a legacy for those we leave behind. Or, at the very top of Maslow's pyramid, for enlightenment. It's just that if we aren't clear about what inspires us most deeply, what we want our lives to stand for in the highest order, our most primal fears, lower level needs and superficial desires will override our deepest ones. As the saying goes, if we don't stand for something, we can fall for anything.

The ever-growing levels of depression and workplace disengagement are testament to this. Millions of people got out of bed this morning and went to work to do a job they feel little or no passion for beyond the money it provides and with no real plan to change their situation. They'll do the same tomorrow. And the day after that. For many, it will continue this way through the best years of their lives as they count down the days until their retirement. Ignoring the siren call of their souls, they sacrifice their deepest longings on the altar of status and security.

It's why living a deeply fulfilling life begins by getting real about what we want it to stand for. Too often the biggest life decisions people make (from the career they pursue to the person they marry) are guided more by what is expected or expedient than by what lights them up. It's why so many people live their lives by default rather than by design, semi-sleepwalking through each day with a general sense of malaise. The noise of their busy industriousness drowns out the quiet voice emanating from the depths. Unsure of what they want their life to stand for beyond the outward success our culture exalts, their desire to look good and feel safe overrides any aspiration for contribution and soul-level satisfaction.

It's why the universe has somehow conspired to land this book into your hands. To expand and fortify your highest aspirations lest your life inadvertently be shaped by your smallest fears.

In *The Road to Character*, David Brooks wrote that 'the central fallacy of modern life is the belief that outward success, with all its grand accomplishments, can produce deep satisfaction'. It's why we have ever more the means to live, but ever less the meaning to live for. With no clear sense of purpose, our smallest fears and desires lead us down the path of least resistance, maximum comfort and lowest risk. A path that never ends anywhere inspiring.

By virtue of the fact that you are reading this now, in your heart you know that you want to live a life that lights you up: a life that is more than getting by, more than looking good, more than feeling comfortable or fitting in.

You might not be sure what it is—yet—but what I know in my own heart as I write this now is this:

You want to live a life that matters; to leave your own imprint on the world for the time you're graced to be here.

It's why investing time to get clear about what you want your life to stand for will lead you on a path to more authentic happiness. (So if you haven't yet grabbed a pen, now's the time!) Because no book, no coach or expert authority or bestselling guru can ever know what is the best path for you. You alone hold the answers you've been searching for. It's just that sometimes you have to do a little more work to dig down to find them, and have a little more patience than you've been endowed with (I speak from experience here!).

Time will march steadily on regardless of whether you are pursuing a vision that inspires you or mindlessly moving through the motions each day on autopilot. Getting clear about the highest vision for your life—what you want it to stand for—will help you lay your vulnerability on the line for something more important. It will guide your choices, fuel your bravery and enable you to keep sight of the big picture when the pressures of daily living threaten to pull you down into the micro-drama of each 'screenshot' along the way.

YOUR INNATE DESIRE TO BELONG, TO LOOK GOOD AND TO FEEL SAFE WILL ALWAYS BE IN A CONSTANT TUG OF WAR WITH YOUR DESIRE FOR GROWTH, CONTRIBUTION AND SELF-EXPRESSION. SUCH IS THE HUMAN CONDITION. ONLY WHEN YOU ARE COMMITTED TO STAND FOR A PURPOSE GREATER THAN YOURSELF WILL THE BIGGEST AND BRAVEST PART OF YOU EVER RISE UP.

Whatever you can do, or dream you can, begin it. Boldness has genius, power and magic in it.

GOETHE

HOW WILL YOU MEASURE SUCCESS?

How successful are you? Your answer, of course, will depend on how you measure success. Chances are the yardstick you've been using is one that has left your moments of feeling truly successful few and far between. If so, then consider that it's because you've unwittingly bought into a definition of success that doesn't serve you and never will. One that is not based on feeling a deep sense of meaning, but one based on what you think you're supposed to accomplish (own, look like, wear, earn, know...) first. Defining success by external markers leaves us living life on a treadmill...forever striving, yet never arriving...or not for long.

Today we have more luxuries, bigger homes, nicer cars, better health and a greater abundance of conveniences than our parents—much less our grandparents—could ever have imagined in their childhood. Yet we are no happier and we feel no more successful. In fact, many people feel less so. A study from Princeton University that analysed Gallup-poll data found that once we have enough income to live on (estimated at a US $75 000 household income in 2010), greater material wealth has diminishing incremental returns on our sense of wellbeing and success. The more pleasures we can afford, the less we tend to savour them.

Of course, it's hard not to be drawn in by the magazine covers, glossy ads and curated imagery bombarding us at every turn. Certainly there's nothing wrong with wanting the corner office, a fabulous body, attractive partner, prize-winning children, professional recognition, ocean views or, heck, our own private island! Nothing at all. Personally, I'd quite like a private jet. With a shower. It's just that when we measure our success by external measures, we set ourselves up to spend our entire lives feeling like we've never made it. Because even when we do, the gloss soon fades and we shift the goal posts that land us back on the treadmill. And on it goes...Only one island? Make it three!

It's why the most important definition of success is the one you create for yourself, not the one others—from your parents to your boss to luxury marketers—may have been pressing on you. It's also essential to define success in a way that doesn't make it contingent on things that lie outside your control, but rather on what lies inside it. It should align to your deepest values and draw out the best of who you are, but also enable you to feel good about yourself when your best efforts don't produce your desired outcomes (which, let's face it, can be a little more often than most of us would like).

Doing that requires getting crystal clear about what living a truly authentic and meaningful life means for you. Creating your own personal yardstick for living your own best life on a daily basis—one that's not dictated by your smallest desires and biggest fears, but by your highest aspirations and deepest values. Like integrity, leadership, courage, kindness, compassion, community, generosity, love, truth, faith, friendship and service.

Winston Churchill once said that true success is moving from one failure to the next without losing enthusiasm. What he didn't say was that these failures must also be in the service of something more important than our ego, status, pride or power. A cause that is greater than just ourselves—a cause that infuses meaning into the everyday activities of our lives; compels us to do what is right over what is easy; and fuels our commitment to lean in, stand up and press on in the face of the forces pulling us to lean out, sit down and give up.

REDEFINE SUCCESS

The questions that follow are intended to help you get clear about your deepest values: about what true success means to you. So get your pen out and let it roll wherever it wants.

Put yourself in the shoes of you at 100 years of age and imagine that a journalist is interviewing you for an article. Write down how you would respond to their questions.

What core values have I tried my best to live by?

What's the single most important decision I've ever made?

How have I impacted the lives of the people around me?

In what ways have I been a role model for others?

What is the most meaningful thing people could say that would reflect my life well lived?

What was my greatest learning from my biggest disappointments?

What is the bravest thing I've ever done?

Given my answers above, as I think about my life today, how can I redefine what it means to be successful so that I can feel a deeper satisfaction and greater success more often than I do right now?

(For instance: 'I am successful every day that I work towards ... [insert your highest vision, bravest goals, values and so on]'.)

KNOW YOUR 'WHY'

Many times, fresh off long-haul flights from the other side of the world, I've gone to drive a car only to find myself sitting in the passenger seat. Then, once correctly planted behind the wheel, I've turned on the wipers when I've meant to indicate changing lanes. It always reminds me that at our core, we are creatures of habit and can easily find ourselves going through the motions of life on autopilot: doing what we've done countless times before without thinking about why we're doing it or whether it's actually working. Which is why clarifying your big 'why' is a critical first step towards figuring out the 'hows'.

Without a 'why', you can end up living permanently in the passenger seat, driving in circles and wondering why you're not moving forward.

'So, what do you do?'

It's a question you've probably been asked many times. Perhaps you have a quick answer. You're an accountant, entrepreneur, academic, designer, architect, recruiter, teacher, consultant, home maker, project manager, professional clown, aspiring rock star…

Or, maybe you don't.

Maybe, like me, you've often struggled to answer that question because no one 'hat' really describes what you do. Yet whatever it is that you do, the label you give it is never as interesting, nor as important, as why you do what you do. Your 'why' changes everything and impacts everyone around you.

When I tell people my passion is helping people find the courage to lead more meaningful lives, it can ignite curiosity. If they want to know more, great. If their eyes glaze over, that's okay too. The only thing that really matters for me is that I'm clear about why I spend so much of my 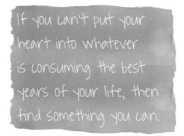 time engaged in my work—as a coach, speaker, writer, mentor, women's advocate, facilitator and media commentator (like I said, lots of hats!).

Knowing your 'why' may not change *what* you do each day, but it will profoundly change *how* you do it—the spirit you bring to the tasks at hand, the people you interact with and the space you inhabit (from your office to your home). As I explored in *Stop Playing Safe*, people who have a clear 'why', even those in menial jobs, outperform those who don't. They're also much better company!

ALL WORK – INCLUDING THAT WHICH WE OFTEN SEE AS LOW-GRADE, DULL OR EVEN 'DIRTY' WORK – HOLDS INTRINSIC VALUE, FORGES CHARACTER AND IS GOOD FOR THE SOUL.

So, if you are not yet willing or able to change *what* you do each day, you can always change *how* you do it. After all, while what you do matters, it's how you do it—the spirit you bring—that matters most of all.

why — DECIDE THE HIGHEST **PURPOSE** FOR YOUR LIFE. **WHY** ARE YOU HERE? (**VALUES**)

how — CLARIFY **HOW** YOU WILL FULFIL IT (**VISION**)

who — COMMIT TO **WHO** YOU WILL **BE** ALONG THE JOURNEY (**VIRTUES**)

what — KNOW **WHAT** YOU WANT TO ACHIEVE (**ACTIONS**)

WHAT'S MY BIG 'WHY'?

So...why am I here? Why does what I do matter?

Don't judge whatever pours off your pen. Just start writing and trust that whatever shows up on the page is perfect.

LIVE ON PURPOSE

Each of us is born to impact the world in some way: to leave it better off because of how we've chosen to 'show up' and the way we've touched the lives of those we've encountered along the way. As Mother Teresa, now Saint Teresa, once said, 'Not all of us can do great things, but we can all do small things with great love'.

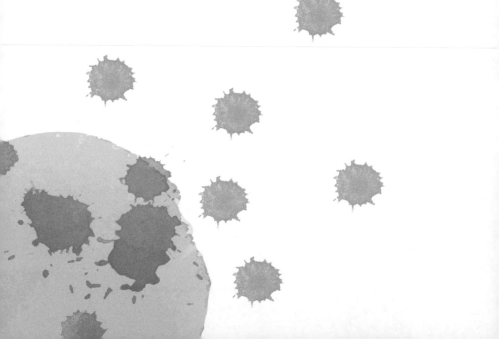

As I write this, my oldest son Lachlan is studying hard so he can pursue his passion for social justice as an international human rights lawyer. I admire his clear sense of purpose and as his mother I'm immensely proud of him. At his age, all I knew was that I wanted to leave my parents' farm and explore the world. Getting a business degree seemed like a good idea, but beyond that, I had no strong sense of mission. Nothing like Lachlan's.

Over the years my sense of purpose has evolved as I've worked to shed my childhood baggage—an eating disorder, bad body image and scarcity thinking—and dealt with the heartaches and hardships I've faced since. Losing my youngest brother Peter after a long battle with mental illness, supporting my oldest brother Frank to adapt to life in a wheelchair, all while figuring out how to conquer my own fears and insecurities and trying not to burden my four kids with them! Time will tell how well I've done.

While some people have a clear sense of purpose early in their lives, most don't. In fact, many people find this whole 'purpose caper' a little unsettling. It's because they let their preconceived notions of what it is to have a purpose—grand and gallant causes such as finding a cure for cancer, ending world hunger or saving endangered species—make them think that they have no real purpose.

But that's not true.

More often, your purpose will unfold, morph and evolve as you move through the seasons of your life and discover more about yourself, the world and how you are uniquely positioned to improve it. So don't get caught up thinking you have to make yourself a contender for the Nobel Peace Prize.

All that matters right now is that you're open to the possibility that you're here, right now, to serve a purpose more important than gratifying your ego or serving yourself and that every experience you've had—every lesson learned, hardship endured, problem solved…and unsolved—has equipped you to make a more meaningful mark than you ever could otherwise.

You can't force your purpose (it won't let you!), but if you sit with the questions that follow, you may gradually get a clearer sense of what life expects of you and the role you're here to fill, however humble or huge it may seem.

> How may I best serve? Imagine what a different world we'd live in if we all woke up each day intent on serving the world as best we could.

For what is far worse than failing is succeeding at something you don't care about.

Whatever you do, don't doubt your power to positively impact the world. After all, when you doubt your power, you give power to your doubts. That just leaves everyone worse off.

Your purpose lies at the intersection of what you're good at, what you care about and what you can do to serve the world—directly or indirectly.

What I'm good at

What I can contribute

What I care about

your purpose

What am I good at?

These are things you've been good at all your life—things that others have always sought you out for, even if you thought nothing of it, and may go all the way back to when you were young. These are your innate strengths and talents—gifts you didn't ask for but somehow got anyway. Along with your natural talents will be things you've become good at: for example, skills you've learned from your career and life up to now, and expertise you've acquired from both formal education and the 'school of hard knocks'.

What can I contribute?

There are many problems, challenges and unmet needs in the world to be solved or filled. You are positioned to help do that in some way. When you get clear about the value you have to bring, and learn how to communicate clearly, others will appreciate you more (which may also be reflected in the money they pay you for what you do). The truth is that the more you can help others get whatever it is they want most (to increase their pleasure or to reduce their pain), the more you'll be able to get what you want most. As Albert Einstein once said, 'Try not to become a man of success, but rather try to become a man of value'.

What do I care about?

We don't all get fired up about the same things. What is it that lights a fire in you? It could be something you're passionate about or something you're angry about; something that excites you, makes you come alive or that you feel needs to change. It may be a childhood dream that never goes away. Include here things you would enjoy doing even if you weren't paid for them, plus things you see others doing that may have triggered a little envy. What matters is that you feel a strong emotion about whatever you write down!

Now write your answers on the next page.

FIND MY PURPOSE

The things I'm good at: What are my strengths, talents, skills and areas of expertise? How do I help other people be more successful and happy? What insights and hard-won wisdom have I gained?

The things I can contribute and add value to: How can I be of greatest service? What wants, needs and desires do I see in the world that I'm able to meet or fulfil? What problems can I help to solve? Where can I help others avoid suffering or enjoy more happiness or success?

The things I care about: What stirs my spirit, ignites my curiosity, makes me come alive? What causes I care about deeply, including those which might make me feel angry?

ACCEPT THE CALL TO ADVENTURE

Adventures are, by their very nature, crowded with uncertainty. Alas, we humans are, by our very nature, wired to avoid them.

We love to make plans based on a future we can predict; to minimise the unknowns and maximise the sureness.

Yet only when we surrender our plans and open wide our arms to the greatest of all adventures (often called 'life'), can we discover our one true source of security and come to know how little we ever needed to fear.

In *The Hero's Journey*, philosopher Joseph Campbell described the deep desire we all have for meaning and purpose. He believed that living out our life's greatest purpose is the true hero's journey—one shared across cultures and over millennia.

Our journey begins when we decide that we cannot go on as we have been because the life we are living is not worth what we're giving up to have it. In making the decision that something must change we are taking up Campbell's 'call to adventure'.

While living a life of adventure is fraught with uncertainty, by daring to go where we have not yet been we discover new horizons of possibility, uncover new strengths and infuse a deeper dimension to our living. In the process we learn the irony of uncertainty:

RISKING OUTRIGHT EXPOSURE SPARES US MORE ANXIETY THAN OVERCAUTION EVER CAN. A LIFETIME SPENT TRYING TO AVOID UNCERTAINTY DOESN'T LEAVE US MORE SECURE, IT LEAVES US LESS SO.

Of course, accepting 'the call' and embracing your life as a wild adventure ride is only one way to see it. The truth is that your life is whatever you decide it to be.

A melodrama.

A comedy.

A precious gift to be savoured or a marathon to be endured. It's all in your mindset.

LIVING YOUR LIFE AS AN ADVENTURE WON'T JUST EXPAND YOUR EXPERIENCES *IN* LIFE. IT WILL CHANGE YOUR EXPERIENCE *OF* LIFE.

Sooner or later we all reach the end of our human journey. Don't wait until the end before you open your arms wide to all that it has to offer you. Doing so will help you find humour amid your hardships and discover within yourself boldness, brilliance, grace and grit you wouldn't have otherwise. In Helen Keller's words, 'Life is a daring adventure or nothing at all'.

EMBRACE THE ADVENTURE

If I were to see my life through the eyes of an adventurer, what new possibilities would open up for me?

How would it shift my day-to-day experience of being alive?

What would I say to myself when things don't go to plan?

MY LIFE MANIFESTO

The message I want my life to stand for is ...

The purpose of my life is to ...

I choose to define success as ...

Embracing life as an adventure opens me up to ...

To make my biggest mark on the world, I need to be someone who ...

SET YOUR COMPASS

LIKE A SHIP ADRIFT AT SEA, WHEN YOU'RE UNSURE WHERE YOU WANT TO END UP, YOU RISK DRIFTING ALONG THE PATH OF LEAST RESISTANCE AND LANDING IN A PLACE YOU'D NEVER CONSCIOUSLY CHOOSE. LIVE BY DESIGN, NOT DEFAULT.

Time is a great equaliser. No matter how hard we may try, we're all gifted with the same 24 hours in a day, seven days in a week, 52 weeks in a year.

So why is it that some people accomplish so much over the course of their lives and others so little? Is it their sharp mind, good looks or good luck?

Hardly. (Plenty of people endowed with all these qualities do very little.)

It's their clarity.

They know what they want, they know why they want it and every decision they make, every day they work, is aligned towards it.

CLARITY = POWER

So too, the clearer you are about what you want (what your 'ideal' looks like in *every* area of your life), the better equipped you'll be to prioritise your time and channel your resources to make it a reality.

In your career, your marriage, family, friendships, finances, body or business—wherever you lack clarity about what you want—your power is diluted. Your power to make smart decisions and set clear boundaries. To tap resourcefulness and grow resilience. To build collaborative relationships and expand influence. To identify opportunity and be an inspirational leader in your workplace, your family and far beyond.

IT'S WHY PEOPLE WHO HAVE NO IDEA WHAT THEY WANT SOMETIMES END UP IN A PLACE THEY DON'T MUCH LIKE.

If you've found yourself some place you may never consciously have chosen (and let's face it, who hasn't?), it's okay. Truly. You've learned some valuable lessons that have brought you to reading this right now. Lessons you can apply to chart a better course for your future.

While you can't change what has happened in the past, every day is an opportunity to decide whether you want to keep moving along in the same direction or to reset your course on a better one. It begins by getting clear about what it is that you want and, sometimes equally important, about what it is you *don't* want. Not anymore anyway.

If you think about it, it really is just common sense that to live your ultimate life you must first decide what 'ultimate' actually looks and feels like for you. After all, how can you create an amazing life that is rich in all the things you desire most—whether it be a rewarding career, a fun and loving marriage, adventure travels, close friendships, radiant energy or a lifestyle you love—if you haven't identified what it is?

You can't.

Having a vision for your life acts as a compass to guide the decisions you make each day. The people you will spend time with and those you won't! The challenges you'll take on and the opportunities you'll turn down. The invitations you'll accept and those you'll decline. The time you'll set your alarm clock to get up and when you'll get home for dinner. What you'll put into your mouth and how you'll take care of your body.

Live your life by design, not default.

IN ANY AREA OF YOUR LIFE WHERE YOU DON'T HAVE A CLEAR VISION OF WHAT YOU WANT YOU HAVE UNCONSCIOUSLY SURRENDERED POWER.

In step 1 you painted the boldest vision for your life. But big dreams without a plan of action can often end up as just that. Wishful thinking. It's why step 2 is about drilling down and creating meaningful goals over three timeframes—short, medium and longer term. Doing so will bring your purpose to life and plug you in to the most potent source of power you'll ever have … the one that flows within you!

> Dreams without a plan of action are just wishful thinking.

Ten years from now all sorts of people, no smarter or better connected than you, will have done all sorts of amazing things that have changed lives and improved the world in some way. (Just think how much amazing stuff has been done in the past 10 years!) If you would like to be one of them, now is your time to decide what you want that future to look like and to set sail towards it.

A year from now you'll be so glad you did.

If you do not change direction, you may end up where you are heading.

LAO TZU

BEGIN WHERE YOU ARE

Let's face it, sometimes pulling back the curtains and confronting the truth of our lives is uncomfortable ... if not downright confronting. Far easier is to keep pretending we've got it sorted, hurtling through life so fast we never stop long enough to examine it. Which is why right now—today—is the best day you'll ever have to audit your life and get real about the price you'll pay if you continue doing more of what isn't serving your highest good.

In the busyness of our day-to-day life it's easy to be pushed along by inertia and a false sense of urgency as we juggle the many pressures, priorities, expectations and responsibilities of our over-scheduled lives. Yet our bias towards the familiar can keep us doing more of the same, rather than stopping to reflect on whether it's actually making us happy or whether it's just what we know.

And at what cost?

Charting your best course through life is not a one-off event in which you reset your internal GPS coordinates—get hitched…raise kids…make the C-suite…pay off the mortgage…run a marathon—and press 'go'. Even if you've been relatively successful up to now, continuing to thrive requires regularly checking in with yourself that you're staying true to yourself: living in alignment with your values and pursuing the highest vision you have for yourself (and if you're unhappy, revising it!).

Many people excel at avoiding the hard work of living well. They find all sorts of ways to distract themselves from the less pretty reality of their lives, which can threaten their ego and the well-crafted image they've curated for the world. They justify destructive behaviour, rationalise irresponsibility, downplay its consequences and come up with a colourful array of explanations to avoid the pain of confronting the truth. Easier to airbrush it away and post another selfie to Facebook. Or so it can feel. As Marianne Williamson wrote in *The Shadow Effect*, 'It takes courage to deeply look at ourselves, but we can't have real freedom and peace until we do'.

JUST AS WEEDS LEFT UNTENDED IN A GARDEN CAN CROWD OUT THE FLOWERS, THE PROBLEMS THAT WE DON'T OWN WILL EVENTUALLY OWN US.

Given how high the stakes are, taking a few minutes right now to do an honest audit of your life can provide a lifetime pay-off. After all, delay has a way of growing increasingly expensive and even what's comfortable now won't stay comfortable forever.

HOW'S MY LIFE LOOKING?

Time to do a little life audit by giving yourself a rating in each of the eight areas of your life as represented in the Wheel of Life below. Rate yourself a 10 if that area is absolutely brilliant and could not be any better. Rate yourself a 0 if it couldn't be any worse. You'll probably give yourself a score somewhere in between. Then colour each segment out as far as the score.

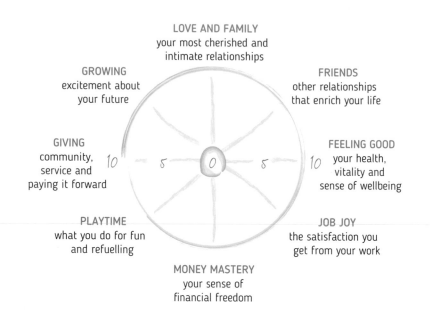

LOVE AND FAMILY
your most cherished and
intimate relationships

GROWING
excitement about
your future

FRIENDS
other relationships
that enrich your life

GIVING
community,
service and
paying it forward

FEELING GOOD
your health,
vitality and
sense of wellbeing

PLAYTIME
what you do for fun
and refuelling

JOB JOY
the satisfaction you
get from your work

MONEY MASTERY
your sense of
financial freedom

What would need to be different in each of the areas in the Wheel of Life for me to give them a solid 10 (or at least a strong 9)?

Love and family: My sense of connection and the intimacy I have with the key people in my life:

Friends: The fun and fulfilment I get from the people I work and socialise with:

Feeling good: My sense of physical wellbeing, vitality and how I feel about my body:

Job joy: How valued I feel through my work and how much I enjoy doing it:

Money mastery: My relationship with money, how wisely I spend it, save it, invest it and my freedom to enjoy it:

Playtime: What I enjoy doing when I'm not working: how much fun do I have?

Giving: The contribution I make to my community and those less fortunate than me:

Growing: How inspired and excited I feel about my future:

PAINT YOUR BOLDEST VISION

Your life expands in direct proportion to the size of the vision you create for it. Yet the bigger your vision, the greater the chasm you have to cross and the higher the risk you'll fail to bridge it. It's why so many people dial down their ambitions, lower their sights and deride dreaming as child's play. It's safer that way. At least in the short term. But sheltering yourself from the possibility of failure confines the size of your life and sucks passion from your days. In which case, you fail by default.

When my husband, Andrew, turned 50, our family decided to climb Mt Kilimanjaro to mark the occasion. My four teenage children had never climbed a mountain before, much less one of the world's seven summits. So it's fair to say we may have been a little naïve in our ambition. A few mountain climbing friends clearly felt we were. Yet we set off to Tanzania intent on making it to the top.

Come 'summit day' we found ourselves struggling for breath and battling nausea and headaches as the altitude took an increasingly steep toll on our bodies. Determined not to give up, we pressed on, one gruelling step after another until, nine hours after setting off from base camp, we arrived at the summit, nearly six kilometres up in the African sky.

WE LEARNED MANY LESSONS FROM OUR CLIMB UP MT KILIMANJARO – ABOUT GRIT, TEAMWORK AND PATIENCE. BUT THE MOST VALUABLE OF ALL WAS LEARNING THAT IT IS ONLY WHEN WE DARE TO TEST OUR LIMITS THAT WE EXPAND THEM.

Living your best life begins with daring to create a vision for your life that exceeds your current capacity to achieve it; one that excites you even as it scares and stretches you.

Right now you have the opportunity to make bigger plans than you've made up until now. Will that itself take courage? You bet. It's why you must create a vision for your life that is so  inspiringly bold that your desire to achieve it will dwarf your fear that you can't.

Make no small plans. You must think bigger to become bigger.

Whatever vision excites you, just keep in mind that we don't all dream of building business empires, helping the vulnerable, performing on stage, climbing mountains, writing books, designing clothes, taking our start-up public or creating artistic works of beauty. That's because we were each born to fulfil a different purpose, to make our own unique mark on the world. I'm not here to make yours and you're not here to make mine. Likewise, if you hold back from daring to make your own mark, many people's lives will be the poorer because of it.

IF YOU DIDN'T HAVE IT WITHIN YOU TO MAKE MANIFEST WHAT IGNITES YOUR IMAGINATION, IT COULD NEVER GET A FOOTHOLD THERE TO BEGIN WITH.

At the end of life most people regret far more the things they didn't do than those they did. They regret living the life others wanted for them instead of the one they wanted for themselves. They regret living too safe, risking too little and giving up on their dreams too early.

IN THE GRAND SCHEME OF LIFE, WE FAIL FAR MORE FROM OVER-CAUTION THAN WE EVER DO FROM OVER-DARING.

You are made for more than comfort and safety and keeping house and looking smashing. You are here to make a mark that no-one else can. The only hitch is that you will only make it if you're willing to fail in your attempt. As author William Shedd once wrote, 'A ship is safe in harbor, but that's not what ships are for'.

In her book *On Purpose*, Karen James says that our vision is the tangible manifestation of our purpose—and the bigger, bolder and more colourful it is, the better.

Dare to paint a bold vision. Dare to set sail towards it. Dare to discover a whole new world.

Chances are, you will do just that.

DARE TO UNLEASH YOUR IMAGINATION

To give your imagination a little wind beneath its wings, let's play a game of 'make believe'. Pretend that you've found a magic wand that holds the power to grant you anything you want if you're willing to do the work required to make it happen.

Anything.

Now, with an invisible magic wand in one hand and your pen in the other, write down what your 'dream life' would look like – and hold nothing back.

Nothing.

The magic you most yearn for in your one-and-only precious life is riding on the courage you have right now to dream a vastly bigger dream for yourself than you may have ever dared to dream before.

Here's a little prompt to get you started. But feel free to ignore it! (This is your life, not mine!)

If I could create for myself the life that inspired me most deeply, it would ...

COMMIT TO ACTION

When you set your stake in the ground and commit to specific goals, it serves as a compass from that moment on: guiding your choices, narrowing your focus and channelling your efforts.

Yet the highest purpose for setting a goal is not the goal itself. It's what it makes of you as it moves you from hoping and wishing to daring and doing.

If you've ever made a new year's resolution late on 31 December only to have your resolve evaporate before Valentine's Day, you'll know that *setting* a goal and *achieving* a goal are two entirely different things.

There are countless books on how to achieve your goals. Of all the tips they hold, one of the most proven and powerful is committing to your goals in writing. Hence the saying, 'Don't just think it, ink it'!

The importance of both creating specific goals and writing them down has been demonstrated time and time again. Most recently, a study by Dr Gail Matthews, a psychology professor at Dominican University in California, found that you are 42 per cent more likely to achieve your goals just by writing them down.

WRITING DOWN WHAT YOU WANT TO ACHIEVE GLUES IT INTO YOUR PSYCHE, CEMENTS YOUR RESOLVE TO BRINGING IT TO REALITY AND SPURS YOU TO STEP INTO – *AND STAY IN* – ACTION OVER THE LONG HAUL.

The best way to accomplish your big, brave vision is to break it down into smaller goals that you can achieve on the not-so-distant horizon. Now is the perfect time to do just that: to set yourself three goals you'd love to accomplish over three different time horizons between six months and five years:

1 *The close horizon (6–12 months):* more specific, with specific actions you will take through to completion.

2 *The near horizon (18 months–3 years):* specific, but with fewer detailed action steps beyond 12 months. These goals will require giving up something you value now for something you'll value more. Scheduling time towards them on a regular basis will be important.

3 *The mid horizon (3–5 years):* less specific, but something that moves you towards fulfilling your biggest goals and highest purpose in the most powerful way. The initial steps may be

specific, but for now the most important thing is that they are laying the groundwork for the future. It could be learning new skills, broadening your network or working towards a long-term passion project. Because these goals are more distant, you'll need to be more disciplined about prioritising time for them each week.

While each goal has a different timeframe, it's important to revisit them regularly. So schedule time in your calendar every three months to review your goals and identify key targets for the next 90 days. It will take you less than an hour, but it will ensure every hour after that is better spent. We'll touch on this again in step 7.

Equally important is how you articulate your goals. Using a modified version of the traditional SMART goal acronym introduced by leadership guru Peter Drucker in the 1980s, ensure your goals contain all of these five attributes.

- *Stretch*—your goals must stretch you beyond your current reach. If you can achieve a goal with little effort, make it bigger!

- *Measurable*—ensure you can track your progress and define success. To quote Drucker, 'You can't manage what you can't measure'.

- *Aligned*—your outward actions should be congruent with your inner intention, so make sure your goals align with your values and highest purpose.

- *Risk*—nothing worthwhile is achieved with a guarantee of success. Make your goals so inspiring that even if you fail, you won't regret having tried.

- *Timely*—set a specific 'done by' date and assign deadlines for key actions and milestones. As stated earlier, this should include revisiting your goals at least quarterly.

We'll touch on this again in the final part of this book.

MY THREE HORIZON GOALS

Horizon goal no 1: What do I want to accomplish within the next 6 to 12 months? Why is it worth my effort?

Horizon goal no. 2: What do I want to accomplish within the next 18 months to 3 years? Why is it worth my effort?

Horizon goal no. 3: What do I want to accomplish within the next 3 to 5 years? Why is it worth my effort?

The first step
towards getting
somewhere is to decide
you are not going to
stay where you are.

JP MORGAN

BE-DO-HAVE

You have an important mission to fulfil. Yet even reading this now might make you feel weak at the knees as you question whether you have what it takes to fulfil it.

The truth is that any quality that you've ever admired in anyone else also resides in you. Life simply hasn't compelled you to find it, much less to develop it.

Now is your time. To test yourself, to invent yourself and to begin embodying the traits you've often wished you had but assumed you didn't.

Every single day of your life you have the opportunity to reinvent yourself. That's not to say that your past hasn't shaped who you are or that some of your personality traits aren't more innate or pronounced. It's simply that through the power of a single decision you can be more of whatever it is you choose to be more of.

More tenacious. More trusting. More determined. More confident. More focused. More organised. More disciplined.

EACH ONE OF US HAS A LITTLE BIT OF EVERY HUMAN VICE AND EVERY HUMAN VIRTUE.

Sure you may have practised some traits more often than others. But that doesn't mean you can't strengthen a behavioural trait if you're committed to practising it.

So as you think about the vision that excites you most, ask yourself who you need to be to accomplish it.

Pulling from the list on the next page (though don't be limited by it), write down four 'power virtues' that you need to embody.

MY POWER VIRTUES

Using the list below, circle the four power virtues you need to embody at this point in your life if you are to achieve your goals and create the life that inspires you most deeply. Feel free to include others.

Accepting	Easygoing	Optimistic
Adaptable	Encouraging	Passionate
Adventurous	Enthusiastic	Patient
Affectionate	Faithful	Peaceful
Ambitious	Flexible	Persistent
Assertive	Focused	Playful
Bold	Friendly	Positive
Collaborative	Generous	Purposeful
Committed	Gracious	Reliable
Compassionate	Grit	Resilient
Considerate	Honest	Resolute
Courageous	Intentional	Self-assured
Daring	Kind	Strong
Deliberate	Loving	Tenacious
Determined	Mindful	Trusting
Disciplined	Open-minded	Unwavering

You may want to write these on a sticky note and pin them around your home office. You can also change them around whenever you feel it would be helpful, but I recommend focusing on no more than four at a time for at least 90 days.

MY POWER VIRTUES IN ACTION

Now, as you think about your top goals or the biggest challenges you're facing in your life right now, ask yourself:

What would I do right now if I were being ... (*virtue 1*)?

What would I do right now if I were being ... (*virtue 2*)?

What would I do right now if I were being ... (*virtue 3*)?

What would I do right now if I were being ... (*virtue 4*)?

Repeat these questions to yourself whenever you find yourself feeling stuck, frustrated or unsure of how best to proceed.

MY BIG, BRAVE GOAL PLAN

By... *(Insert a specific date 6–12 months from now.)*

I will have ...

which will make me feel ...

....

By... *(Insert a specific date 12–18 months from now.)*

I will have ...

which will make me feel ...

....

By... *(Insert a specific date 18 months to 3 years from now.)*

I will have ...

which will make me feel ...

....

The power virtues I will embody are ...

1.

2.

3.

4.

UPGRADE YOUR MENTAL MAPS

BEYOND WHAT YOU CAN CURRENTLY SEE LIES A FIELD OF VAST POSSIBILITIES – FOR CONNECTING AND CREATING; FOR SERVICE, SELF-EXPRESSION AND SOUL-LEVEL SUCCESS. YOU HAVE NO IDEA WHO YOU CAN BE UNTIL YOU REWRITE THE STORY YOU'VE TOLD YOURSELF ABOUT WHO YOU ARE.

A few years back, a Japanese tourist visiting Australia drove her rental car straight into the Pacific Ocean. When later asked how this happened, she explained that she was just following the car's GPS and 'it told me I could drive down there'. You could put it down to her being a foreigner in a strange country, but then that wouldn't explain the Canadian local who followed her car's GPS right down a boat launch into an icy cold lake. As her car became submerged she was able to escape out a window and swim to shore. She declined media interviews. I would too.

As you probably know yourself, there are plenty of stories just like these. (Perhaps you've even had your own close encounter with a lake.) They serve to highlight an important distinction for successfully navigating any journey:

The map is not the territory.

The same is true for life. We all have our own internal 'GPS' system: mental maps we rely on to help us navigate life. What we often forget is that our mental maps aren't actually reality; they're just our representation of it. Yet because we follow them as though they were, they shape our relationships, our careers and, ultimately, direct the course of our lives.

Many of your mental maps do precisely what they're supposed to do: help you get from your current Point A to your desired Point B. For instance, to enjoy more love (and less conflict) in your relationships, raise responsible kids, stay healthy, create financial freedom, move forward in your business or career and handle setbacks along the way.

If they do, these maps are working *for* you.

Other times, particularly when you find yourself in unfamiliar territory like our Japanese tourist, your maps can give you a bum steer ... like into an ocean!

These maps are working *against* you!

Needless to say, your mental map of the world isn't always accurate. Nor is it complete. Sometimes you might look at a situation and think, 'That's it!' when in fact there's a whole lot more territory and options available to you that you aren't even aware of.

YOU SIMPLY DON'T KNOW WHAT YOU DON'T KNOW.

Maybe you know someone whose map of the world is small and simplistic. Someone who mistakenly thinks they don't have any other options but to live the way they do, when in fact there are many other options available to them. They're just blind to them. Because they 'don't know what they don't know' they live a far smaller life than they could, and regularly make choices that only perpetuate their problems and sabotage their own happiness.

People with limited mental maps stay in jobs they loathe and relationships that leave them lonely because they think there's no other way. They often refuse to try something new because their map stops abruptly at the end of their comfort zone (which generally isn't very big!). So they keep doing the same thing over and over, even when it's getting them nowhere and making them miserable, because their mental map has them believing there's no better way.

OF COURSE, IT'S EASIER TO SEE WHEN SOMEONE ELSE IS USING A FAULTY MAP THAN WHEN YOU ARE. IT'S WHY ONE OF THE MOST IMPORTANT LESSONS YOU CAN EVER LEARN IS THAT YOU DON'T SEE THE WORLD AS *IT IS*, YOU SEE IT AS *YOU ARE*.

Your current mental map landed you where you are today. Yet even if you're largely happy about where you are, because the world is always changing, your current mental schemas will be insufficient to help you build the life you want to be living five years from now, much less 25.

Your map may seem like an accurate representation of your reality, but it's not. Nobody's map is ever fully complete. There is always something to learn and there is always something to unlearn: a belief, an assumption or a story that is limiting you in some way.

Likewise, if you're constantly coming up against the same sort of problems dressed in different outfits—relationship conflict, work stress, over-commitment, too few real friends, yo-yo weight, financial anxiety—chances are the map relating to that aspect of your life needs some tweaking... if not a total overhaul.

So, in step 3 we're taking a look at how you're looking at life. We'll identify some of the assumptions, beliefs, biases and 'stories' that make up the mental map you've been using to navigate your way to here, and look at how to rewrite the stories that aren't working for you. Or, put another way, to upgrade your internal GPS! We're also going to dive a little deeper into three of the more common components that comprise the stories you tell yourself—your 'shoulds', excuses and labels—and that can limit where you go and who you become.

BY TAKING A LOOK AT HOW YOU'RE LOOKING AT LIFE YOU'LL BE ABLE TO UPGRADE YOUR MENTAL MAPS TO CHART A BETTER AND BRAVER PATH FORWARD – IN YOUR WORK, YOUR RELATIONSHIPS, YOUR LEADERSHIP AND LIFE.

It begins with having the courage to own the fact that you alone are the author of your life and that you alone must take responsibility for rewriting the stories that have held you back, blinkered your thinking and kept you repeating the same cycles of thinking that are not serving you and never will.

If you're ready to start a new chapter, now is the time. You ready?

To map out a
course of action and
follow it to an end
requires courage.

RALPH WALDO EMERSON

WRITE YOUR OWN STORY

You are a story-making machine. You have a story about everything. Who you are. How you were raised. What you're good at. What you're lousy at. What you can achieve and what's stopped you having it already.

There's nothing inherently wrong or right about the stories you tell yourself. Rather, they are either expanding what is possible for you or they are shrinking it. Either way, any area of your life that isn't moving closer to what you want holds a story in need of rewriting.

Albert Camus once wrote that our lives are the lump sum of our choices. The challenge we all face is to make smart choices and avoid foolish ones. Doing that requires constantly challenging and updating your mental schemas about what it takes to achieve what inspires you, to change what doesn't, to meet your challenges and to respond to those who challenge you.

Any area of your life where you've found yourself continually feeling a level of dissatisfaction holds a story that isn't serving you (and perhaps it never did). That's because the stories you tell yourself either amplify the positive emotions you feel each day or they do the opposite—grow tension in your relationships, trigger anger, amplify your fears and sabotage your efforts to get ahead and make your mark.

In fact, your story may actually be keeping you from knowing you have a mark to make! Like the one I used to have that, 'you can't be a great mother and have a great career'. Thanks to a wonderful coach, I let go of that story—if I hadn't, you wouldn't be reading this now!

EVERY STORY YOU CREATE, CREATES YOU.

Of course, it's not the circumstances of your life—past, present or future—that shape you, but the story you are telling yourself about it. The story you are *still* telling. The story you will continue to tell until you get real about what it's costing you to keep it.

Our stories have a profound impact on our lives. Every day, our stories amplify our emotions and direct our actions, large and small. Over time, they determine the trajectory of our lives. For instance, the story you are telling yourself right now will determine whether or not you might decide to...

- pick up the phone and risk rejection
- introduce yourself to someone you really admire (whose success may be intimidating to some)
- ask someone to help you out with something
- volunteer to lead a project or committee

- turn down an opportunity or invitation you might once have jumped at because it will distract you from bigger aspirations

- call someone out for treating you (or someone else) with a lack of respect

- admit you made a mistake and say you're sorry.

Each of these decisions is impacted by the story you tell yourself about who you are, about how the world works and about other people—those you know and those you don't. Certainly, any time you feel intimidated by someone, therein lies a story that's limiting you!

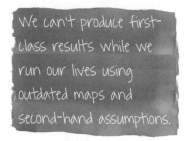
We can't produce first-class results while we run our lives using outdated maps and second-hand assumptions.

While many of our day-to-day decisions may seem relatively inconsequential, they rarely are. Every decision has a consequence; each has the power to open doors or close them, to build trust in a relationship or undermine it, to grow self-respect or surrender it to self-interest.

Yet challenging our stories requires effort we often prefer not to make. We are masters of self-deception and often unconsciously pick and choose the evidence we use to justify the story we've created. The Reticular Activating System (RAS) in our brains makes us hardwired to be this way: to actively seek out evidence that supports our beliefs (what psychologists have called 'confirmation bias') and to actively tune out, or deny, evidence that refutes it (coined the 'perceptual defence mechanism'). It explains why people with strong political

If your story is making you miserable, change it.

affiliations can be completely blind to compelling evidence that supports an opposing perspective. Their map simply can't incorporate information that doesn't buttress their ideology.

IT'S A TRUE TEST OF COURAGE TO CONFRONT THE TRUTH ABOUT THE MISTRUTHS WE TELL OURSELVES; TO OWN OUR INNATE BIAS FOR KEEPING THEM ALIVE.

To create positive change in any area of your life you need to dig beneath the actions you've been taking to the story underneath: a story that is triggering and amplifying the negative emotions which are impairing your actions.

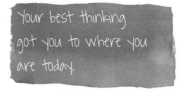

Your best thinking got you to where you are today.

ONLY WHEN YOU EXAMINE THE STORY YOU'RE TELLING YOURSELF ABOUT A PROBLEM, PERSON OR YOURSELF CAN YOU DEAL WITH IT BETTER.

In *Loving What Is*, author Byron Katie wrote that, 'everything outside you is a reflection of your own thinking. You are the storyteller, the projector of all stories, and the world is the projected image of your thoughts'. If you ever tell yourself that you aren't smart enough, you'll never get ahead, you're destined to be lonely, your boss hates you, your parents failed you or you're too old to change, then I can tell you right now that you're living inside a story that's holding your future hostage.

To create a future that is filled with more of what lifts you up and less of what weighs you down, it will pay to challenge your stories again and again and again. Let's get to it!

MY STORY

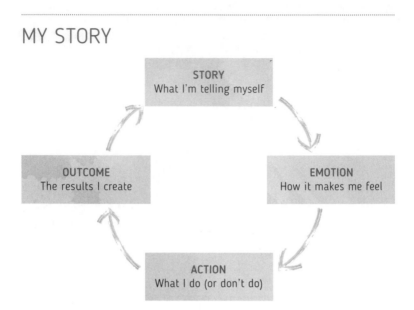

Think about something that isn't as you want it to be. Then go through the following steps.

Clarify your story

Where have I cast myself as a victim, others as villains or blamed a past event or person for a current problem?

Gauge its impact

How has this story made me feel? What emotions has it triggered and does it continue to amplify for me?

What actions have I taken (or not taken) as a result of feeling this way? Has my story kept me from dealing with this situation more constructively and courageously?
(*Hint: If you're unhappy with the outcome, your story isn't working for you!*)

Who could I be and what might I do if I weren't living in this story?

Consider alternatives

How might the wisest person I know or ever admired (living or dead) look at this situation? How does this shift how I feel about it?

Write a new story

Tapping the biggest and bravest part of myself, what new story will I tell myself that frees me of the constraints of my old one? Write it down, beginning with 'My new story about this is ...'

Notice how it shifts how you feel and what you see is possible.

What possibilities open up for me if I tell myself this story? What will I do now that I wouldn't have done before?

SHELVE YOUR 'SHOULDS'

Too often we buy into the unwritten rules and societal norms about what we *should* and *shouldn't* do. Like what we *should* study, who we *should* marry, where we *should* live, how we *should* raise our kids and live our lives.

Yet our 'shoulds' are often far more about *other* people's values than about *our* values and what we actually want for ourselves.

It's why we must neither 'should' on ourselves nor let others 'should' on us.

If you've ever been relieved or even delighted when someone cancelled a dinner engagement, then you've experienced the impact 'shoulds' can have on your life. Like thinking you should say yes to an invitation because you know it will please the person extending it and not because you actually want to spend an evening with them.

Our lives are filled with 'shoulds':

You should study hard and go to university.

You should honour tradition and be close to your family.

You should aim for the C-suite and take no prisoners as you go.

You should settle down and have a family.

You should stay home with your kids.

You should have 10 per cent body fat.

You should pursue a secure career.

A subset of our stories, our 'shoulds' are a melting pot of social expectations, familial rules, tribal values and cultural norms. They are neither right nor wrong. Rather, they serve us, enabling us to live more connected and rewarding lives, or they don't.

IF YOUR 'SHOULDS' OFTEN LEAVE YOU FEELING GUILTY, STRESSED, CONFLICTED OR RESENTFUL THEN MAYBE IT'S TIME TO STEP BACK AND LOOK AT WHERE YOU ARE 'SHOULDING' ON YOURSELF OR LETTING OTHERS 'SHOULD' ON YOU.

You'll know it's time to break away from the 'shoulds' when your desire to make yourself happy overtakes your desire to keep everyone else happy. It takes courage to live life on your own terms. It begins by taking a look at where you've been letting what others expect of and want for you matter more than what you want for yourself.

OUR 'SHOULDS' ARE UNQUESTIONED RULES WE UNCONSCIOUSLY BUY INTO THAT BLINKER US FROM SEEING OTHER OPTIONS. IT'S WHY PEOPLE WHO LIVE 'SHOULDIE' LIVES CAN NEVER LIVE BIG ONES.

The very word 'should' generally has far more to do with what we think is expected from us than what we truly want for ourselves. 'Should' carries with it an implicit judgement that one course of action is inherently better than another. For instance: it's better to be a doctor than a nurse; it's better to live close to family than in another state (or country); it's better to have a Luis Vuitton handbag than one from Kmart.

It's why you've likely been told at some point where you should go to university, buy your home or send your kids to school. Or how you should raise those children, manage your career or spend the dollars you earn from it.

The question to ask yourself is this:

IS WHAT YOU ARE GETTING FROM DOING WHAT YOU THINK YOU SHOULD BE DOING WORTH WHAT YOU'RE GIVING UP IN THE PROCESS?

To help avoid the latter and give you more freedom in the choices you're making, you can replace the word 'should' with the word 'could' and include other options. For instance, instead of 'I should stick it out with this job two more years to build up a resume' you could say 'I could stick with this job or I could start looking for a new one right now'.

Likewise, in your relationships you likely have a whole lot of 'shoulds' that you are imposing on others. Your boss should stop putting so much on your plate. Your neighbour should water your plants while you're away. Your husband should buy you flowers on your birthday. Your kids should keep their rooms tidy. Your mother-in-law should stop telling you how to raise *your* kids.

Who says they should?

Who says anyone should do what you think they should do? This is *your* problem, not theirs! Yet if you stick with your 'shoulds' you can drive wedges into your relationships, get yourself bent right out of shape and pull others down with you.

JUST IMAGINE THE STRESS YOU WOULD SPARE YOURSELF IF YOU LET GO OF THE BELIEFS ABOUT WHAT PEOPLE SHOULD AND SHOULDN'T DO; ABOUT WHAT *YOU* SHOULD AND SHOULDN'T DO!

Make your own rules. Live by your own values. Forge your own path. Let others do the same. Anything else sets you up for a life of stress, resentment and, ultimately, regret.

DON'T LIVE A 'SHOULDIE' LIFE

Think about an area of your life that isn't working for you – or is continually causing you to feel angst, resentment, frustration or simply a lack of satisfaction – and reflect on these questions.

Where have my actions been driven by what I have thought I should do versus what I've really wanted to do?

What payoff have I gained from doing what I felt I should do versus what I really wanted to do?

What price have I paid for doing what I felt I should do versus what I really wanted to do? Where has it left me resentful?

If I let go of what I thought I should do and just did what I truly wanted to do, in ways consistent with my deeper values, what would I start doing and what would I stop doing?

PARK YOUR EXCUSES

Listen to the excuses of truly successful people and one thing will stand out: they don't make any. That's because people who live big lives don't trade in excuses. Rather, they own their choices and take full responsibility for the results they create, what they do and what they don't. So too must you.

If you really want to do something, then do it. If you don't, that's cool. Just stop lying to yourself about why you haven't already.

I'm too busy. I'm too old. I'm too tired.

I'm not a morning person. I wouldn't know where to start. I haven't got the money.

I'm just not disciplined/outgoing/experienced/educated/connected/ (fill-in-the-blank) enough.

There's an old saying that if you want to do something you'll find a way and if you don't, you'll find an excuse. It's true. Excuses are really just masterfully engineered 'reasons' we tell ourselves—and anyone else in earshot—to justify our actions or, more often, our inaction. And let's face it, there'll never be a shortage of convenient reasons to defend your inaction.

You are busy. You haven't done it before. You're not as supported as you'd like. It is difficult. You could fail. The sky might fall in too. One never knows. Not really.

THERE WILL ALWAYS BE AN ABUNDANCE OF READILY AVAILABLE REASONS TO JUSTIFY YOUR LOT IN LIFE AND WHY YOU'RE UNABLE TO IMPROVE IT.

Certainly you will always find people to back up your excuses. Of course, they won't be the doers and go-getters. Those people won't stand for them. No, they'll be the ones who tend to trade in excuses themselves to explain why aspects of their own life aren't as they want it to be either. As Benjamin Franklin once wrote, 'He who is good at excuses is rarely good at anything else'.

BUT HERE'S THE DEAL: THE QUALITY OF YOUR LIFE IS SHAPED BY THE QUALITY OF YOUR EXCUSES.

This may sound harsh, but most of the excuses you've been making are simply ways to cover up for the fact that either:

- you really don't want to do something (you think you 'should' but you don't really want to…not enough anyway)

or

- you're really just afraid that if you try you'll fail, so why make all that effort?

More often than not our excuses are just lies wrapped up as reasons to avoid the real work of living our best life. Yet you and I know that you are better than that. So if you're ready to be done with the excuses that have not been serving you and never will, now is the time.

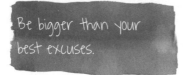

Be bigger than your best excuses.

EXCUSES BE GONE!

What excuses have I been making?
(*List each excuse for each area of your life that you couldn't rate at least a 9 in your life audit.*)

What's the price I will pay if I keep trading in these excuses?

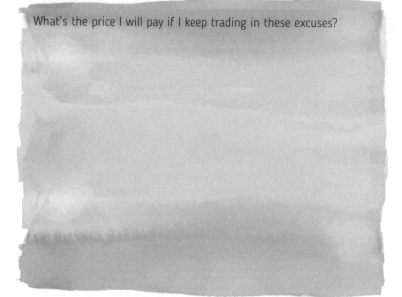

What is a more powerful choice I can make for each excuse?
(*For example, 'I just don't want to do this' could be 'I will do this!'*)

Courage is the price that life exacts for granting peace.

AMELIA EARHART

LIMIT YOUR LABELS

Some labels can be helpful. Ones like 'Caution: Poisonous'. Others ... not so much.

The labels we apply to everything from our job to our body to our personality and proficiency can box us in, building mental boundaries we never venture to cross. It's not that the labels themselves are dangerous. It's that once we've bought into them, we don't challenge their validity.

Just imagine who you could be if you peeled off the labels you've been walking around in up to now. The sky would become your limit. Not your labels.

The labels you use to describe yourself, other people and situations can, at times, be helpful.

You're a nature lover. A life-long learner. A go-getter.

Your family is close. Your friends are fabulous. Your life is blessed.

Your job is demanding but rewarding. Your future is exciting.

All well and good. But too often, the labels we apply to ourselves and others can confine us.

I'm not a morning person. A control freak. A couch potato.

She's crazy. He's lazy. We're doomed.

My work is stressful. My business is ruined. My life is a nightmare.

When we treat these labels as truths they prevent us knowing anything else. Our reality conforms to our labels. Our experience of life becomes a nightmare. Our business can only be doomed. Our marriage can never be joyful. Our job can only be stressful.

Which is simply, totally and completely *untrue*.

WHO YOU ARE IS NOT THE LABELS YOU HAVE APPLIED TO YOURSELF, YOUR SITUATION OR YOUR FUTURE. YOU ARE FAR MORE THAN ANY ADJECTIVE.

Neither are the people around you the labels you may have slapped on them. They may have acted in ways that befitted that label, but they are not their label. They are capable of being more and different and better. Just as you are.

Just because you've never been good at something doesn't mean you can't get better. Just because you failed last time doesn't mean you're a failure. Just because you lost the job doesn't mean you're a loser and just because you often feel lazy doesn't mean you can't get out of bed an hour earlier and get some serious stuff done!

REMOVE THY LABELS

What labels have you given yourself that have limited how you've seen yourself?

What possibilities would open up for you if you removed these labels?

MY LIFE, MY STORY

Old story

The old story I've been telling myself is that...

This story has left me feeling...

and kept me from...

New story

The new story I am telling myself is that...

This story makes me feel...

and inspires me to...

It is never too late
to be what you
might have been.

GEORGE ELLIOT

EXIT THE SAFE LANE

THERE IS NO SHORTCUT TO CREATING A LIFE WORTH LIVING EXCEPT BY EMBRACING UNCERTAINTY AND CHOOSING GROWTH OVER COMFORT. AGAIN AND AGAIN AND AGAIN. BE UNAFRAID OF BEING AFRAID. LIVING BRAVELY IS INDISPENSABLE FOR LIVING WELL.

Let's face it, if it were easy to do the right thing, the brave thing, the best thing...the very thing that you knew would move you towards more of what you wanted and away from what you didn't, you'd already have done it. And you wouldn't be here now. Neither would I, for that matter.

As I've learned many times over the course of my life, fear is a potent emotion. Left unchecked, it can derail our decisions and keep us living in the safe lane of life: the lane that often doubles as a parking lot for unfulfilled dreams and unused potential.

Couple our innate risk aversion with the fact that we live in a world that's constantly bombarding us with reasons to feel afraid—of killer viruses, rogue terrorists, identity theft and predators of every variety—and it's little wonder that so many people spend so much time in the safe lane of life.

OUR CULTURE INSTILS FEAR INTO OUR VEINS FROM BIRTH.

Yet at what cost?

If your definition of success from earlier in this book has anything to do with living a life that lights you up, brings out your best and makes life better for others, then achieving success—in your career, relationships, health, wealth and life—will be determined by how willing you are to discern the fears that are serving you from those that are stifling you; to trade the familiarity of what you have now for the possibility of what you want most.

Some people choose not to do that. It makes them anxious. It feels too scary. They'd rather do coffee, watch reality TV, or post selfies or photos of their dinner—all just more of what already leaves them hungry and falls short, far short, of setting their soul on fire. They've plenty of company to affirm their choice. The endless stream of selfies on your average Instagram feed and the ratings for (un)reality TV are testament to it.

Many people spend years of their life (if not decades) staying in situations that neither nurture their strengths nor ignite their spirit. Their immediate need to feel safe or significant now wins out over their deeper desire to feel fulfilled later. The status quo may not light them up and their passion may dry up, but hey, at least their future is certain and they don't have to sweat the possibility of failing or losing face or being left alone.

Or so they tell themselves.

IT MAY SOUND COUNTERINTUITIVE, BUT PEOPLE WHO OPT TO STAY WITH THE FAMILIARITY OF THE STATUS QUO DON'T GROW MORE CONFIDENT OVER TIME. THEY GROW LESS SO.

Their sense of security is fragile and hangs on nothing and nobody changing around them and everyone continually affirming their worth (or 'like'-ing those selfies!). Since it doesn't come from within them, they cling to certainty and resist anything that threatens it. Yet all certainty is mere illusion. Anyone who thinks they have it is kidding themselves and on a one-way path to some form of breakdown.

If you've stopped counting the candles on your birthday cake, you'll know that change is a permanent condition. As such, true security can only ever be found within us, never outside of us, particularly not in the objects we surround ourselves with. Your only true source of lasting security comes from knowing that within you lie all the resources you need to deal with whatever changes life holds in store for you—that whatever happens, you can handle it.

It's why courage is the first among all the virtues—because, to quote Aristotle, it is the one and only virtue that guarantees all the others. The courage to have faith in yourself, to embrace life's inherent uncertainty and to move towards the highest and most inspiring vision for your life, regardless of how inadequate you fear you may be to achieve it.

> Courage may not guarantee success but it always precedes it.

The courage to exit the safe lane for the brave lane.

In the end there is no substitute for courage: for simply having the guts to declare that while you feel afraid about what could go wrong, you are going to take a bold leap of faith towards the future that is calling you. You are going to breathe into those butterflies doing backflips in your belly. You are going to embrace the knot in your chest or the lump in your throat. You are going to feel your fear and proceed right through the heart of it.

One thing is certain: people who are willing to embrace discomfort as a prerequisite for living a deeply meaningful life not only go further, but they enjoy this magical mystery tour of life immeasurably more than those who don't. The exercises and questions in the chapters that follow are designed to help you do just that.

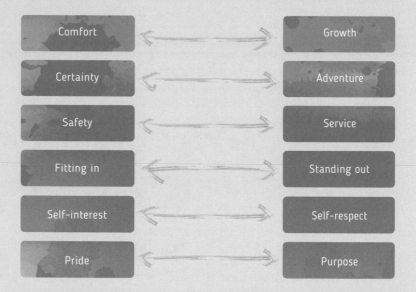

Twenty years from now you will be more disappointed by the things you didn't do than by the ones you did do.

MARK TWAIN

FEARLESS

Growing up on a farm riding horses, I learned early on that growth and comfort can't ride the same horse. It's why the things you want most – in work, love and life – are riding on your willingness to trade the comfort you have now for the fulfilment you want most.

In the end, there is no substitute for courage; no shortcut to bravery. To be the person you most need to be in order to create the life you most yearn to live, you must commit to embracing discomfort and doing the very thing that often scares you most. Again and again and again.

As a human being, you were not put on this earth to get by. Nor were you born just to 'look good' or 'stay safe'. You came into this world to grow and learn and blossom into the fullest possible version of the person you have it within you to be. To make a mark that no-one else can make … not exactly. There's just one catch:

You cannot live your biggest life without getting uncomfortable.

Of course, our safety zone (often called the comfort zone) has no defined borders. It's unique to each of us. What's exciting for one person—parachuting, performing, public speaking—is terrifying for another. So exiting your safety zone doesn't mean stepping so far out you become paralysed with terror. Let's face it, that would just be dumb. It simply means stepping into your 'courage zone', stretching yourself, challenging yourself and, as you go, becoming more comfortable feeling uncomfortable. Because (and here's the good news!) courage is like a muscle: the more you use it, the stronger it gets and the less afraid you feel.

AS YOU GROW MORE COMFORTABLE WITH BEING UNCOMFORTABLE, FEWER THINGS WILL SCARE YOU. IT'S BY ACTING AS THOUGH YOU FEEL FEARLESS THAT YOU START TO ACTUALLY FEAR LESS.

Let me add a caveat in here though.

Your safety zone is not to be avoided entirely. As I'll discuss in the final part of this book, there are times you need to retreat to where you feel unthreatened, safe and nurtured to refill your tank, recharge your spirit and recover from loss. It's why sustained periods of fighting fires and forging new ground that can deplete your energy must be balanced with activities that restore it.

You just have to be careful you don't spend so much time doing what's easy and unchallenging that you start languishing. By its very nature, your safety zone is not a place where you can thrive. Live, get by, relax, recharge, keep up appearances, escape or just live a Stepford Wife life of immaculate mediocrity? Sure.

But thrive? Impossible.

The only thing that truly matters is that you recognise the vital importance of trading growth for comfort as often as is necessary for your own authentic happiness. Odds are, it will be more than you feel like, but never more than you can handle!

The seven steps of my Fear*Less* Framework will help you reclaim the power that fear holds in your life and use it as your ally. I'm not promising to eradicate fear from your life (let's face it, that could be hazardous!), but rather to help you fear less: owning your fear, taming your fear and stepping through it to whatever is waiting for you on the other side.

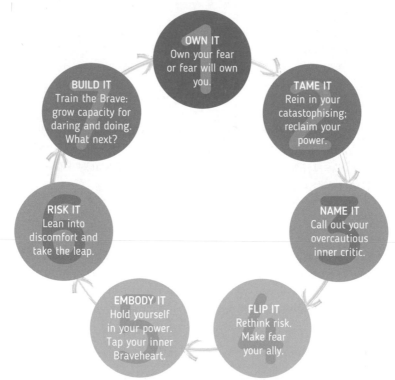

If you're ready to embrace discomfort as a prerequisite for living well, the seven chapters that follow and the exercises they contain will open up a whole new world of possibility for you.

The desire for safety stands against every great and noble enterprise.

TACITUS

OWN IT
WHAT YOU RESIST PERSISTS

Maybe you're scared to death of not amounting to anything: of never reaching the stars you've dreamed about. Maybe the thought of being alone leaves you cold. Maybe you fear you'll be rejected by your friends or humiliated in front of your peers. That your kids will abandon you or that the market will crash. Again.

Or perhaps what scares you most is you'll never be 'enough' – successful enough, smart enough, loveable enough, good enough, worthy enough. That, sooner or later, even those who admire you will realise you aren't all they thought – that you're really an imposter masquerading as someone else. Someone better. Someone who knows what they are doing.

Maybe 'All of the above'.

If simply thinking about any of these things triggers a dull sense of dread, then your fears are alive and well—as they are for most of the other three billion people you share this planet with.

Fear is a potent and primal emotion. It's wired into your psychological DNA to keep you safe and protect you from harm. All good stuff. It's just that if you aren't vigilant, fear can set up permanent residence in your life. Without realising it, you become inured to it to the point where your fear steers the reins of every decision and taints every interaction, until you forget what it was ever like to live without it.

IN TODAY'S CLIMATE OF FEAR, WHERE WE'RE CONSTANTLY REMINDED OF THE DANGERS LYING IN WAIT FOR THE UNWARY, WE HAVE TO BE EXTRA DISCERNING NOT TO ALLOW FEAR OF ALL THAT COULD GO WRONG KEEP US FROM TAKING THE VERY RISKS NEEDED TO MAKE THINGS MORE RIGHT.

Yet if it were easy to step through your fear, risk mistakes and expose yourself to the very things that stoke your anxiety—whether that be losing your job, your home or your friends—everyone would do it.

There is no magic formula (or 7-step book!) to permanently liberate you from fear. Nor would it serve you if there were. Fear has a role to play.

YET WHILE FEAR WORKS TO KEEP YOU SAFE, IT CAN ALSO KEEP YOU LIVING TOO SAFE. IT'S WHY YOU HAVE TO OWN YOUR FEAR LEST FEAR OWNS YOU.

Whatever you resist will always persist. The things we fail to own and acknowledge about ourselves ultimately find a way of showing up in our lives, often unconsciously. So confronting the truth about what scares you most is an essential first step towards reclaiming the power it has held over you.

OWNING YOUR FEAR BRINGS IT OUT OF THE SHADOWS AND INTO THE LIGHT. THAT ALONE CAN SEND THE MONSTERS PACKING.

Likewise, by denying fear or pushing it away, it buries deeper and its shadow grows longer. As long as you fail to dig down to uncover your deepest fears they will continue to weigh you down and rob you of your freedom to create the life you want for yourself.

IF THERE'S ONE THING I'VE LEARNED FROM YEARS OF LIVING IN THE SHADOW OF FEAR, IT'S THAT LIVING ANY PLACE ELSE IS NOT TRULY LIVING AT ALL.

OWN YOUR FEAR

Think about what you would love to achieve or change in your life.

What fears have kept you taking action already? Write them down. Drill down beneath the surface level. Get to the core of the fear that's held a stranglehold over you ... trace it back to its roots. At the deepest level, what scares you most?

TAME IT
STOP
CATASTROPHISING

Our imagination is a wondrous thing. Without it, the most beautiful works of human kind would never have been brought into existence. Perhaps you wouldn't have been either! Yet when fuelled by fear, our imagination can drive us to underestimate ourselves, overestimate the risks and exaggerate potential consequences. By turning shadows into monsters, it can fool us into believing that danger lurks around the corner and that we're safer staying exactly where we are.

So you want to make a change, or take a chance or shake things up a little … or a lot. But *arghhhh* … what if everything goes wrong?

What if I mess things up?

What if I misjudge the situation?

What if people let me down?

What if I fall short?

What if it turns into a complete and utter unmitigated disaster … like you end up homeless, totally broke, abandoned by your friends, disowned by your family, the laughing stock of everybody you've ever wanted to be respected by?

Fear drives you to focus more on what could go wrong than on what could go right.

WHAT IF …?!

Let's face it, for all the beauty our imagination can conceive, when fear takes hold of it, it can come up with some pretty worrisome, if not outright terrifying, scenarios.

It's called 'catastrophising'. (Well that's what I call it anyway.)

It can freeze you in your tracks and guarantee you never fail because it stops you ever daring to attempt. In novelist Stephen King's words, 'Monsters are real, and ghosts are real too. They live inside us, and sometimes, they win'.

It's little surprise that most of the things we spend our lives afraid might happen never actually do. Our children aren't abducted. We don't catch the killer virus. Our plane doesn't crash.

> It's not the event that you fear that holds the power over you; it's your fear of it.

Fear is the by-product of the thoughts you create in your own head; the projection of some possible future occurrence fuelled by an experience from the past. Usually one that is completely disconnected.

FEAR is an acronym for False Evidence Appearing Real. Taming it sometimes requires figuring out whether our 'monsters and ghosts' are real or just figments of our imagination kept alive from our past. After all, it's not what you *think* you fear, it's what you *link* to fear.

THE IRONY IS THAT IN OUR EFFORTS TO AVOID 'THE WORST' WE OFTEN INADVERTENTLY CREATE MORE ANXIETY THAN WE WOULD HAVE HAD WE RISKED FULL EXPOSURE.

Not only that, but we pay a steep opportunity cost as we deprive ourselves of building the confidence, courage, capacity, competence and sheer enjoyment we gain when we dare to do more than we have before. Little wonder people blessed with abundant wealth who do nothing meaningful with it can end up being so depressed. They're missing the juice of life that is extracted from being stretched and challenged.

COURAGE ZONE
where you grow confidence, competence and capacity for greater
daring and doing. For example: Ask for help. Say no. Say yes. Say 'enough!'
Put yourself 'out there'. Risk rejection. Set a bold goal. Start over.

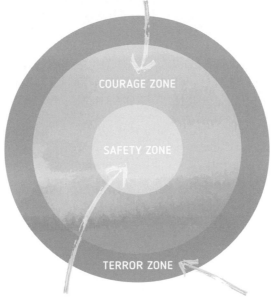

SAFETY ZONE
a good place to recharge and recentre — but don't
stay there permanently lest your 'muscles for life'
wither and you lose confidence for anything else.

TERROR ZONE
where you freeze up
and shut down.
Best to avoid!

By asking yourself what's the worst thing that could happen and then sitting with any fear that rises up, you come to know that even if it did happen, which is often highly unlikely, it would not kill you. Rather, it would introduce you to yourself on a whole new level: you'd learn, you'd grow and you'd emerge from it a wiser, braver and better version of yourself than you were before.

DARING TO EXPOSE YOURSELF TO THOSE MONSTERS IN YOUR HEAD IS ULTIMATELY FAR LESS FRIGHTENING THAN SPENDING YOUR ENTIRE LIFE RUNNING FROM THEM.

When you expose your worst fear to the truth, you open the doorway to a whole new realm of possibility: freedom to dare boldly, to speak truthfully and to live authentically.

EXPOSE THE MONSTERS IN YOUR HEAD

So, as you think about taking the big, bold action towards the future you most want, ask yourself:

What is my absolute worst fear? *(Your worst case scenario.)*

If it did begin to happen, what would I do to intervene and manage any fall out?

What are the outcomes of more probable scenarios? How likely is it that I could produce at least a moderately good outcome?

How are events from my past amplifying my fear of what might happen in the future and driving me to overestimate the risks?

Bravery escapes
more dangers
than cowardice.

JOSEPH-ALEXANDRE PIERRE DE SÉGUR

NAME IT
CALL OUT YOUR INNER CRITIC

Who are you to do that? You don't know what you're doing. What will everyone think? You'll make a fool of yourself. It's not worth it! Better to be safe than sorry.

No-one can escape the inner voice that is our own worst critic, urges caution at every step and preaches pessimism at every opportunity. Yet everyone can learn to relate to it for what it is – the most primal part of our being trying to keep us safe. It just has a rather Neanderthal way of doing it.

The great operatic tenor Enrico Caruso was once struck with stage fright just moments before he was due to walk on stage to perform for thousands of people. As he stood backstage in full costume, totally overwhelmed and despairing, with perspiration pouring down his face, his throat was paralysed. Trembling, he said to those near him, 'I can't sing. They will all laugh at me. My career is finished'.

He turned around to walk back to his dressing room. Suddenly he stopped. 'The Little Me is trying to strangle the Big Me within!' he shouted.

That one moment of courage changed everything. Turning back towards the stage, Caruso lifted his shoulders up straight and with his most powerful voice commanded, 'Get out of here!' to the voice of doubt in his head. 'The Big Me wants to sing through me. Get out, get out, the Big Me is going to sing,' he repeated again. He then walked on stage to give one of the finest performances of his career, which later saw him becoming one of the greatest tenors in history.

IF A LITTLE VOICE IN YOUR HEAD HAS EVER TOLD YOU THAT YOU DON'T HAVE WHAT IT TAKES AND WARNED YOU AGAINST STEPPING INTO THE LIMELIGHT, YOU'RE IN EXCELLENT COMPANY (MY OWN INCLUDED).

While the voice of the Little You can get awfully loud, it's important to remember that it was wired into our 'monkey brain' back in our Neanderthal days and wants nothing more than to protect you from pain, rejection, humiliation and harm.

When your 'inner critic' (as it is so often called) is at its loudest, it's simply because it's feeling the most threatened. So while it may not seem like it's trying to help you, it's really just afraid you'll put yourself in a situation that could compromise your safety, your security, your significance and your sense of identity. As psychologist and author Dr Kristin Neff has said, 'You don't want to beat yourself up for beating yourself up in the vain hope that it will somehow make you stop beating yourself up'.

YOU CAN SPEND A LOT OF TIME BERATING YOUR INNER CRITIC, OR YOU CAN BEFRIEND IT ... AND THEN CALL IT OUT!

The latter may sound counter-intuitive, but reframing how you think about the cautious critic in your head enables you to keep it in its place. One of the most powerful ways to do this is to do what Caruso did: give it a name.

It doesn't matter what you call your inner voice of fear, only that it helps you to realise that you are not your fear and that your fear is not you.

FEAR IS AN EMOTION, NOT REALITY. IT DOES NOT DESERVE TO BE GIVEN THE POWER TO KEEP THE BIG YOU FROM TAKING CENTRE STAGE IN YOUR OWN LIFE.

When the Little You is at its loudest then you need to speak to it as you would anyone whose deep concern for you made them worry about you doing something silly (like an over-protective parent). You acknowledge its concern with kindness, and then, with all the authority you can muster up, let it know who's boss!

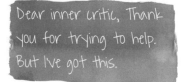

Dear inner critic, Thank you for trying to help. But I've got this.

PUT YOUR INNER CRITIC IN ITS PLACE

Where have I been giving that small voice of fear too much power?

What name will I give the cautious, critical voice in my head? Little Me? Doubting Debbie? Gremlin? Chicken Little?

What will I say to it from now on each time it pipes up and tries to scare me from moving forward and showing up fully?

FLIP IT
RETHINK RISK

We human beings excel at imagining how we might feel tomorrow if we take a risk and things don't work out. Yet we're often lousy at imagining how we'll feel a year from now if we do nothing.

While potential losses loom larger in our imagination than potential gains, taking your best path forward requires being brutally honest about what you are putting at risk if you stay on your current course.

Playing it safe can be a high-risk approach.

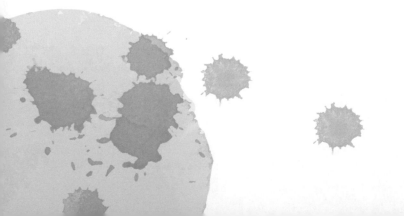

The unknown is always scary. At least a little. Just the thought of doing something we haven't done before can trigger all sorts of fears to rise up and scream a message to our brain: B-E-W-A-R-E.

Sweaty hands. A tight chest. Clenched jaw. Shallow breath. Shaking knees. Restless sleep.

When considering whether to take a risk, we are wired to focus more on what could go wrong than on what could go right. In *Stop Playing Safe* I shared the research behind this, but just know that you are wired to focus more on what you could lose than on what you could gain; on what could go wrong than on what might go right; on overestimating the risks 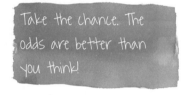 and underestimating ourselves (and if you're a woman, double it!).

Take the chance. The odds are better than you think!

Our risk aversion is all part of the survival instinct: better to stay in the cave with the tribe than head out to be eaten by a hungry sabre-tooth tiger. Until we too become hungry. Yet what we are not so good at is imagining how we will feel further down the road—a year from now, a decade from now, on our deathbed—if we do nothing. It explains why so many people spend the best years of their lives taking the path of least resistance and sitting impassively on the sidelines living what philosopher Henry Thoreau called a life of 'quiet desperation'.

It's also why we sometimes need to turn fear into our ally and ask the question:

What should I fear if I do nothing?

Put another way, if you continue on your current path—complete with its trappings of comfort, familiarity and convenience—what might you one day look back upon and regret not having done with your one and only precious life? While the clinical term for this is 'neuro-associative conditioning', I prefer to call it 'flipping fear': turning fear into your ally by refocusing on what you need to be afraid of if you try to avoid what scares you—like falling flat on your face, your friends' disapproval or being exposed as less capable or 'together' than people may think. I've felt all of these on more occasions than I can count.

You can 'flip fear' by stepping into the shoes of your future self and imagining how you'll feel in the years to come if you let the fear that's undermined your actions until now continue to pilot your life. Visualise yourself staring at your reflection in a mirror 5, 10, 25 years from now if you've allowed your fear of failing or looking foolish continue to keep you from stepping up to the plate in your life, making changes and taking chances.

Don't discount the cost of inaction. Things that aren't working now generally don't get better when left unattended—they get worse. Delay can grow increasingly expensive as it exacts a mounting toll on our health, wealth, career, relationships and life.

HANGING OUT IN YOUR COMFORT ZONE GROWS INCREASINGLY UNCOMFORTABLE.

It's a rule of psychology that for something to change, the pain of staying where you are must exceed the pain of changing it. It's why the intention of the following exercise is to help you connect with the pain you may feel down the track if you choose not to change what is already not working in your life, to pursue that dream or seize that opportunity. Playing it safe can be a high-risk approach.

So, building on the Wheel of Life exercise in step 2, let's do a little cost–benefit analysis on the areas of your life that you rated lowest. To do this you will need to put yourself in the shoes of the 'future you' and imagine how you'll feel five years from now if

Fear regret more than you fear failure.

you play it safe and do nothing. If the thought that things will be the same in five years leaves you cold, then make it one year from now. Just do what works!

As you consider what you can gain and lose, also consider the emotions that you would feel with each outcome, both the immediate emotions and those you'll have to contend with over the longer term if you take that course of action.

Many people tip-toe warily through life with a 'feeling phobia', avoiding situations where they may have to feel anything very deeply. While it can seem like a 'safe' approach to living, avoiding potential lows also cuts off potential highs. So, often it's not the event itself we're afraid of but how we think we will feel if it happens. The very thought of being rejected or losing face in front of our peers can be far more terrifying than the actual event itself.

INSTEAD OF THINKING ABOUT WHAT YOU WOULD DO IF YOU WEREN'T AFRAID TO FAIL, DECIDE WHAT IS SO IMPORTANT TO YOU THAT EVEN IF YOU DIDN'T SUCCEED, YOU WOULD NEVER REGRET HAVING TRIED.

True courage is laying something you value on the line for something you value even more. What are you willing to put at risk—looking good to your friends, feeling safe in your job, your family's approval—because you're unwilling to look back one day and wonder 'What if?' Only you can answer that question, but whatever your answer, be sure that you aren't unconsciously permitting your fear of what could go wrong to override your desire to make things more right.

RETHINK RISK

	Take the risk	Avoid the risk
What I can gain (include not just specific benefits but also the emotions you will enjoy or find comfort in)		
What I can lose (include not just the costs but the emotions associated with them, e.g. regret)		

Put yourself in your shoes 10 years from now. What would my future self want me to do right now?

Go confidently in the direction of your dreams. Live the life you have imagined.

HENRY DAVID THOREAU

EMBODY IT
HOLD YOURSELF
IN YOUR POWER

The capacity for greatness resides within every one of us. Without exception. It's just that some of us have been living inside a story about our own inadequacy for so long that we've become strangers to the bravest part of ourselves.

It doesn't need to stay that way.

Simply by shifting your physiology you can loosen fear's grip and reconnect to your inner Braveheart!

Try this as a little experiment.

Wear a frown, cast your eyes down, clench your fists and teeth, slump your shoulders and let your belly hang loose. Think of something that makes you really mad, really scared or both.

Notice how that makes you feel. Odds are it won't be positive!

Now do just the opposite.

Stand (or sit) tall, as though there were a string pulling up through your head so you are long and tall and strong. Bring your shoulders back. Wear a quiet smile on your face. Lift your chin and look gently upwards. Hold your stomach strong. Place your feet shoulder-width apart, firmly rooted to the ground beneath. Take three big, deep breaths and imagine a time you have felt like you could take on the world. Strong. Capable. Confident. Purposeful. Unstoppable. Breathe into that feeling. Clench your fists and store that feeling there.

Now, connected to your bravest self, visualise yourself doing the very thing you know you need to do to move towards the life you most want; to do whatever has been tugging at your heart for too long. What is it? Where are you? Who are you with? What are you doing? What are you saying? What are you creating? Picture yourself taking bold, self-assured action. Picture the people around you reacting to you as someone who knows their worth and what they want: someone to be admired, to be respected, to be reckoned with.

Feel the power of that moment. Take hold of it. Remember it. Own it. Get ready to use it.

Try it now.

EVERY SINGLE DAY YOU CAN BRING YOUR BRAVEST SELF TO YOUR BIGGEST CHALLENGES. IT BEGINS BY SHIFTING YOUR PHYSIOLOGY AND THEN CONNECTING TO THE BRAVEST PART OF YOU THAT YEARNS TO LIVE THE BIGGEST LIFE YOU POSSIBLY CAN; TO MAKE THE MARK THAT ONLY YOU CAN MAKE.

Own your power. Embrace your truth. Honour your gifts.

EMBODY YOUR INNER BRAVEHEART

When I embody the bravest part of who I am and imagine myself
triumphant, where do I feel called to step up?

We must believe
that we are gifted
for something, and
that this thing,
at whatever cost,
must be attained.

....

MARIE CURIE

RISK IT
EMBRACE
DISCOMFORT!

The more often you put yourself 'out there' – out on the limb where only the big dreamers and darers venture to go; out in front of the very people who can open new doors, buy your wares, test your talent, build your tribe or broaden your thinking – the sooner you'll strike it 'lucky'. Though of course, it won't be luck at all.

Courage may not guarantee success, but it always precedes it.

The idea that people who act with bravery and boldness attract more good fortune is far from new. Yet it holds as much truth today as it did during the heyday of ancient Greece when the phrase *audentes fortuna iuvat*—'fortune favours the bold'—first came into being.

YOU MAKE YOUR OWN LUCK EACH TIME YOU CHOOSE GROWTH OVER COMFORT AND POSSIBILITY OVER PRIDE.

It's simple maths really.

Think of it a little like a gardener planting seeds in a new garden. Each time you take a risk towards what you want, you plant a seed for something really cool to grow. Some seeds sprout fast. Some seeds can take years to germinate into anything worthwhile. Some grow into something way better than you'd ever imagined. And the odd seed is a dud, never sprouting into anything. The thing is, only when you risk planting dud seeds do you grow the odds of planting magnificent ones!

When you're starting out towards something new, it can be hard to discern which risks to take, where best to channel your courage or plant those seeds of possibility and opportunity. It's all new ground and you've yet to figure out where you'll get the best results. So instead of putting all your resources into one option, take smaller risks on different ones. Put another way, plant lots of seeds, in lots of pots, and trust that over time you'll figure out which ones will produce the best payoff.

NOT EVERY RISK YOU TAKE WILL PAY OFF, BUT THE BIGGEST MISTAKE YOU CAN MAKE IS TO HOLD OFF PUTTING YOURSELF 'OUT THERE' UNTIL YOU KNOW EXACTLY WHAT YOU'RE DOING OR YOU FEEL BRAVE ENOUGH TO DO IT.

Your brain isn't wired for blazing new trails, it's wired to uphold the status quo. When you're weighing up whether to veer off the beaten path, a whole host of 'cognitive biases' kick in to steer you back onto it.

PSYCHOLOGIST AND NOBEL PRIZE LAUREATE DR DANIEL KAHNEMAN FOUND IN HIS RESEARCH ON DECISION MAKING THAT OUR BRAINS ARE TWICE AS SENSITIVE TO POTENTIAL LOSSES AS THEY ARE TO POTENTIAL GAINS.

Because we hate to lose more than we love to win, the odds are usually better than we assess them to be. It's why you should back yourself more, doubt yourself less and realise that while every course of action involves risk, inaction has its own risks.

Every decision you make has trade-offs. So don't kid yourself that you're being sensible when actually you're being too cautious. We fail far more from timidity than we ever do from over-daring.

There will never be a perfect time to make the change, take the chance and step towards the future that is waiting for you. But the next best time will be now.

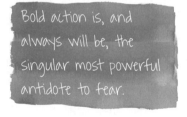
Bold action is, and always will be, the singular most powerful antidote to fear.

By simply daring to take a single step in the direction that inspires you, you send a signal to the universe (but most of all, to yourself!) that you're serious about creating a future that is different from your past. Bigger and better too!

The sooner you start putting yourself 'out there' and taking action to create, achieve and experience what you most want (and change what you *most don't want*), the sooner you'll start to see firsthand that fortune truly does favour the brave.

So don't wait to be discovered.

Don't wait until you're a master.

Don't wait to be given permission.

Don't wait for the universe to send you a message in a bottle or for Mr Right to rock up on your doorstep.

Above all, don't wait until you're 100 per cent sure you can't fail before you take that first exhilarating and terrifying step towards the future that is waiting for you.

Just get started.

Right away.

Like *now*.

THE UNIVERSE WILL DO ITS BIT. BUT YOU HAVE TO DO YOURS.

You have no idea what is possible for you over the rest of your lifetime if you decide, today, that fear has no place at the helm in your life.

Life rewards action.

RISK MORE SUCCESS

If I were going to back myself and step up the plate of my life with the courage needed to hit my future out of the park:

What would I start doing?

What would I stop doing?

Where would I put myself 'out there' like never before?

As you go the way
of life you shall
see a great chasm.
Jump. It is not as
wide as you think.

....

NATIVE AMERICAN PROVERB

BUILD IT
TRAIN THE BRAVE

Courage is a skill, and like all skills, it can be learned and mastered.

It's a little like building up your muscles working out at the gym. In the beginning, even the smaller weights test your resolve. But if you keep showing up, continue practising and don't let discomfort deter you, over time those small weights feel lighter and you find yourself lifting more with less effort.

So too it is in life.

EACH TIME YOU FACE YOUR FEAR AND 'TRAIN THE BRAVE' WITHIN YOU, YOU EXPAND YOUR CAPACITY FOR GREATER DARING AND DOING. BUT THAT'S NOT THE BEST PART. GROWING YOUR MUSCLES FOR LIFE DOESN'T JUST MAKE YOU A STRONGER PERSON. IT EMPOWERS YOU TO LIFT EVERYONE AROUND YOU.

Think back to the first day of your first job. Do you recall feeling nervous or worried that you'd do something wrong and make a fool of yourself? Or worse, get sacked for not being smart enough. But then you started learning the ropes and over time you got pretty good at it. By the time you left you could probably have done it blindfolded. (Or maybe not quite blindfolded, but you get the point.) What once made you nervous no longer did, as the 'hard and scary' had become 'easy and comfortable'. In fact, it was probably a little boring. You looked forward to something new — something bigger and more challenging.

And then you began a new job and went through the whole cycle again, except that this time the challenges that scared you were far bigger than last time. But you leaned in and learned what it took until, eventually, you were ready for something bigger … for more responsibility, more challenge, more change … and on it went.

Well, what if in 30 years' time you could look back at where you are right now: at the challenges that are daunting you or the opportunities that scare you? What do you think the wiser, older version of you might have to say about them?

I'll tell you what they'd say. They'd say this:

Don't wait until you feel brave and bold. Just get out there and act with the courage you wish you had.

Or something like that.

THE TRUTH IS THAT EVERY TIME YOU ACT IN THE PRESENCE OF FEAR YOU DILUTE ITS POWER AND STRENGTHEN YOUR OWN.

Likewise, you build your 'courage muscles' in your work, relationships, leadership and life each time you push through the discomfort and choose to take action despite your fears and misgivings.

Don't feel that you have to take on the world right away. Just as you would not head for the heaviest weights at the gym on your first visit, start building your courage muscles by doing something small. Something that doesn't leave you breaking out in a cold sweat and cowering in the corner in a ball of fear! Rather, decide to do something that's 'a bit scary' or just mildly uncomfortable. Pick up the phone rather than sending an email. Invite someone out. Share an idea. Give some gentle feedback. Write a blog post.

Build your confidence to do bigger things through a series of smaller stretches. With each step outside your comfort zone, you expand your capacity to do more with less angst. Likewise, as you take on more risk you grow your tolerance for risk and your confidence to handle it better. Courage begets courage.

DARE TO BE BRAVE

If I trust that I have all the courage I need to live a deeply rewarding, no-regrets life, what might the very bravest part of me want to say to the part of me that worries I'm not up for to task?

MY COURAGE PLEDGE

I acknowledge that my fears are trying to keep me safe, but that they can also keep me living too safe. For this reason I pledge to:

- **Do what's right over what's easy**, and never surrender my self-respect for self-interest. No matter what.

- **Take full responsibility** for my life, and refuse to blame and indulge in self-pity, which only diminishes my power.

- **Own my unique value** and never talk myself down or let anyone diminish me.

- **Challenge how I look at life** and rewrite the stories I tell myself that keep me stuck, harm my relationships and limit my future.

- **Choose growth instead of comfort** and, when needed, trade the familiarity of the known for the new possibilities of the future.

- **Speak more bravely**, sharing what's weighing me down in ways that respect the right of others to see things differently.

- **Risk making mistakes** and stop waiting until I know everything before I start doing something.

- **Own my individuality** and be myself, no matter how much pressure I feel to fit in and conform to the expectations and norms of others.

- **Forgive myself** when I slip up, fall down and fail to be the person I want to be.

- **Forgive others** for their mistakes (even when they aren't sorry) and let go of the hurts and grudges that chain me to the past.

- **Open my heart wide** to all that life has to offer, and risk the possibility of having it broken in the process.

- **Say 'no' to good things** so that I can say 'yes!' to the great things.

- **Apologise** when I let people down or cause offence, even if unintentionally.

- **Believe that I'm here for a purpose**, and that every challenge is an invitation to grow into the person I was born to become.

LEAN INTO THE CURVES

LIFE DOESN'T HAPPEN *TO* YOU, IT HAPPENS *FOR* YOU. EVERY DISAPPOINTMENT AND DERAILED PLAN IS REALLY JUST A SILENT INVITATION FOR LIVING DEEPER AND GROWING WISER. LIFE IS NOT LINEAR. BY LEANING IN TO ITS CURVES YOU DISCOVER ITS GOLD.

Life is full of curve balls. Some you can sense are coming around the next corner. Others hit you from nowhere. There's no time to duck and it can take hours, days, even months, to reset your bearings and make a new plan.

No doubt you've had your share of curve balls. I'm sure you've also learned that no matter how much you may plan ahead to prepare for every contingency or mitigate against every risk, sometimes, pardon my French, 'shit just happens'.

When it does, it tests you. Will you fall to pieces, rail against the world and throw your own little pity party? Or will you pick yourself up and focus on making the best of your new reality? Or a bit of both?

I've learned that sometimes we have to give ourselves time—a few hours, or days, or weeks—to grieve the loss of the future we'd planned on living. The times I've lost unborn babies. The times my husband has come home to say we'll be moving state, or country, or hemisphere. The times my children have taken a different path from the one I'd imagined for them.

WHEN THE WORLD AS YOU KNEW IT GETS TIPPED OFF ITS AXIS, IT CAN TAKE TIME TO REGAIN YOUR FOOTING BEFORE MOVING FORWARD.

Yet just as the best cars will hug the curves of a winding road, so too you can learn to handle the curve balls life throws your way (and if you haven't had any yet, they're coming!). You may not like them, you could outright loathe them and you will certainly not have prepared for them. But the only way to handle them is to accept them, embrace them and do your best to find the good in them (though this can take time). Because no matter how dire the circumstances may seem or how little control you have to change them, they will always—*always*—hold the seed of some benefit.

CONSIDER THE PERSON YOU WOULD BE TODAY IF EVERYTHING YOU HAD EVER WISHED OR PLANNED FOR HAD TURNED OUT JUST THE WAY YOU WANTED.

If your parents had given you everything you asked for.

If your first crush had declared their undying love and swept you off your feet never to leave your side again.

If you'd won lotto at 18 and never had to work another day of your life, much less those minimum-wage, part-time jobs that helped pay your way through school or your first trip overseas.

If you had never experienced disappointment or fallen short of the mark in any endeavour.

THE TRUTH IS THAT EVERY DISAPPOINTMENT AND DERAILMENT, EVERY SETBACK AND STRUGGLE, EVERY HARDSHIP AND HEARTACHE HAS HELD A VALUABLE LESSON FOR LIVING DEEPER AND GROWING WISER.

You may not have picked up all the lessons quickly. Perhaps, like me, there are still a few that you're working on (we can't be fast learners at everything!). But every one of those experiences you've had that you hadn't planned for, couldn't have anticipated and that may even have knocked you flat to the ground have brought you to where you are today.

So too, every experience that lies ahead offers no less valuable lessons for growing into the full quota of the man or woman you have it within you to be.

If you're up for the learning.

View your problems and 'problem people' through the 'it-shouldn't-be-this-way' lens and they can trigger enormous angst, stress, frustration, fear and bitterness. This is the lens that expects that life should conform to your plans, that bad things shouldn't happen (at least not to good people like yourself), that hard work should always pay off, and that people should do the right thing and see the world as you do.

Ahh, if only.

Viewing life through this lens sets you up for a life of struggle. Of feeling perpetually stressed, upset, pissed off or put out.

But there's another lens, and it's not Pollyanna's rose-coloured glasses.

The other lens views life as though everything that has ever happened, or will ever happen, is conspiring in your favour. Not immediately ... not obviously ... but ultimately.

This lens is forged in faith and optimism and an open mind.

It believes that everything works out in the end and that if things haven't worked out, it's not yet the end.

It knows that 'shit happens', but that it's what you do after the fact that matters far more.

It knows that within every problem lies opportunity.

It knows that every difficult person (and let's face it, there are plenty of them) is a teacher in disguise—someone put in your path to challenge you to think a little bigger, act a little braver, be a little kinder or just become more patient than you may have otherwise been.

IT KNOWS THAT HEARTACHE IS A PART OF LIVING FULLY AND THAT NOT RISKING IT CUTS YOU OFF FROM LIFE'S RICHEST JOY.

It knows that sadness is a natural response to loss and should be embraced, not avoided.

It knows that while you're not always responsible for your experiences *in* life, you're always responsible for your experience *of* life.

And last, but not least, it knows that even when all hope seems futile, there is always a reason to hold onto it and that nothing, and no-one, is ever truly, fully, a lost cause. As I wrote in *Brave* after losing my younger brother Peter, no matter how much we cherish what we have lost, there is a gift that can be salvaged from what remains.

Of course, living life through this lens is not a one-off affair. Old habits die hard and if you've spent much of your life expecting life to be different from how it has been, expecting people to be different from what *they* have been and expecting yourself to be different from what *you* have been, then it will take your full commitment to see your life anew.

But it will be worth it. Because your happiness doesn't correlate with how much your reality conforms to your plans. It correlates with your readiness to accept what cannot be changed, to give your best to improving what can, and to finding that seed of goodness...however hard it may be at first to find.

WHILE OUR PLANS MAY FOLLOW A STRAIGHT PATH, LIFE DOESN'T. IT'S NOT LINEAR. YOU MAY NOT LOVE ITS TWISTS AND TURNS, BUT YOU'LL BE HAPPIER WHEN YOU LIGHTEN UP AND LEAN INTO WHATEVER'S COMING AROUND THE NEXT CORNER.

Investing time to reflect on the questions in the following chapters will help you do just that.

QUIT WRESTLING REALITY

The great 18th-century Prussian field marshal Helmuth von Moltke the Elder once said that no plan ever survives its first encounter with the enemy. The same is true for life.

No matter how brilliant your plans, it's almost guaranteed that something will happen to keep you from executing them exactly as you've envisaged. That doesn't mean you should ditch them altogether. Far from it. It just means it's better to write them in pencil and rework them as often as needed.

This will be more often than you like.

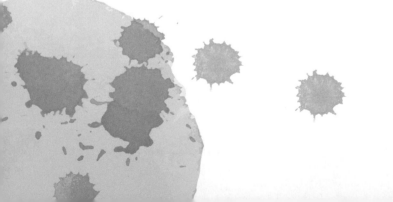

Read the biography of anyone who's achieved anything truly remarkable and you'll discover that their plans went awry more times than they didn't. It's what they did next that set them apart from the pack.

What they *didn't* do was fall in a heap of self-pity, whine incessantly to anyone in earshot, blame bad advice or explain their failure as a permanent inadequacy on their part.

What they *did* do was confront their new reality, take full responsibility for what they did or failed to do that contributed to it, garner whatever insights they could and then reset their sails.

So too can you.

It begins by giving up your fight with reality, complete with finger pointing and complaining about what *shoulda, woulda, coulda* happened. This means giving up the idea that the universe—complete with all those who fly in your orbit—is supposed to fall straight into line with your plans and priorities.

NOT ONLY DO THINGS NEVER HAPPEN IN THE STRAIGHT LINE YOU PLANNED ON, BUT THE BEST OPPORTUNITIES OFTEN APPEAR AS A RESULT.

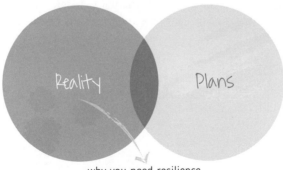

why you need resilience

Of course, it's exceptionally easy to get caught up in focusing on all that's not right in your world—with what you *can't do* or *don't have* or what *would have been better* if only your plans had worked out. It's why so many people excel at it. Yet, as I've learned from a few periods in my life when my plans have derailed, dwelling on what's gone wrong never—*ever*—serves us. It only amplifies existing negativity, fuelling greater resentment, self-pity, blame, remorse or anxiety. All emotions that siphon energy, steal joy and burden relationships. All emotions that keep you from taking the very actions that could improve your future circumstances and find something positive in your current ones.

AFTER ALL, EVERY MOMENT YOU SPEND FOCUSING ON WHAT YOU CAN'T CHANGE IS A MOMENT YOU AREN'T IMPROVING WHAT YOU CAN.

On the flipside, when you accept your situation for what it is (even when it's far from how you'd like it to be) and consciously decide to focus on changing what's within your control, you'll improve your situation and expand your ability to influence what's outside it. For instance, you can reframe things in a positive way, intentionally use 'can do' language, seek out new knowledge, sign up to a class to learn new skills, ask someone for help, get online and do some research, rework your plan and, most important of all, work on yourself (including answering the questions in this book!).

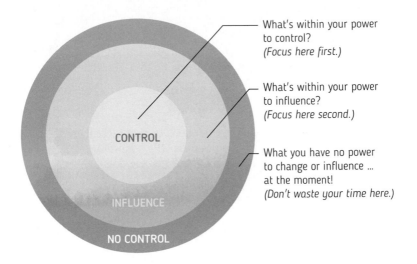

What's within your power
to control?
(Focus here first.)

What's within your power
to influence?
(Focus here second.)

What you have no power
to change or influence ...
at the moment!
(Don't waste your time here.)

CONTROL

INFLUENCE

NO CONTROL

Letting go of your fight with reality isn't about being passive and throwing in the towel on your dreams or surrendering to defeat. Rather, it's not wasting time trying to steer the river, but resetting your sails so you can flow with the current, not against it.

LOVE WHAT IS

Bring to mind a problem you've been struggling to deal with and answer the following questions.

Where has focusing on what has not gone to plan fuelled a sense of resentment, self-pity or powerlessness? (*Be honest!*)

What could be possible if I gave up resisting this problem, both in opportunity and my ability to feel happier despite this problem?

If I decided to stop trying to 'steer the river' and focused on what's within my control, what would I start doing?

What benefits can I gain from having this problem? For instance, how can working on what's within my control turn this problem into a 'win' for me and others?

GIVE YOURSELF PERMISSION TO FAIL

Inventor and industrial designer James Dyson became famous for inventing the dual cyclone bagless vacuum cleaner. Less known is that, while developing his vacuum, he went through 5126 failed prototypes (yes, he counted), exhausting his savings in the process. Like Thomas Edison, who had more than 10000 failed experiments before he discovered how to get the light bulb to glow, Dyson never interpreted his failed experiments as failures. Instead he saw them as yet one more way not to succeed. Today, his net worth runs in the billions.

The singular most important trait that distinguishes people who succeed after failure is this: they never let their failures define them.

Walt Disney started his own business from his home garage and his very first cartoon production went bankrupt. Henry Ford's first two automobile companies also went bankrupt. Stephen King's first book, *Carrie*, was rejected by over 30 publishers. Colonel Sanders of KFC fame had his famous fried chicken recipe rejected more than 1000 times before a restaurant accepted it. Abraham Lincoln, one of the greatest leaders and US presidents in history, had several failed businesses and lost more elections than he ever won.

And remember Virgin Cola? No? Consider it as evidence that not all Sir Richard Branson's ventures turned to gold.

The lesson?

TO BE SUCCESSFUL, YOU MUST GIVE YOURSELF PERMISSION TO FAIL. OFTEN.

Since it is only by risking failure, repeatedly, that you can truly learn what it takes to succeed.

Does that remove the sting of rejection or the disappointment of plans gone awry? Of course not. No-one relishes failure. Yet giving yourself permission to fail keeps you from personalising it: from interpreting it as some permanent and personal deficiency on your part; a sign that you should hang up your hat and never venture off your couch again.

THE REALITY IS THAT NOTHING WORTH DOING COMES WITH A MONEY-BACK GUARANTEE OF SUCCESS. IF IT DID, IT WOULD NOT BE WORTH DOING!

Every story of success holds a tale of bold daring and bouncing back from failure. Sometimes many of them.

Key to failing well is not to spend years dragging it out by repeating the same pattern of failure again and again and again. While Dyson may have failed more than 5000 times to perfect his vacuum cleaner, with each prototype he created he mixed up what he was doing. By figuring out what didn't work, he was able to figure out what would. Same for Edison. If he'd never given himself permission to fail, we may still be living by candlelight.

If you've ever held onto an ill-fitting jacket or pair of jeans because of how much you paid for them, you'll know that admitting you made a poor investment can be painful. It's why admitting failure can take every bit as much courage as pressing on. Just be mindful that doing more of what's already not working in the hope that it eventually will isn't brave, it's foolish.

EVERY DAY YOU CONTINUE INVESTING IN SOMETHING THAT ISN'T MOVING YOU TOWARDS THE OUTCOME YOU WANT IS A DAY YOU AREN'T SPENDING DOING SOMETHING THAT COULD.

But what if you reframed failure as a successful experiment? How might that free you to fail more often, but to fail faster, with less drama and a faster 'bounce back' time? Treating everything you do as an experiment—giving yourself permission to fail—helps you recognise when it's time to cut your losses, to learn the lessons failure holds and, to quote Henry Ford, 'to move on more intelligently'.

Research in positive psychology shows that much of our success in life is determined by how we explain failure (what the father of positive psychology, Martin Seligman, calls our 'explanatory style'). View failure as evidence of your personal inadequacy and you won't risk it nearly often enough (if ever). View it as part and parcel of what it takes to succeed—lessons to be learned, skills to be grown, experience to be gained, resilience to be built—and you'll go further than you ever could otherwise.

As you're considering your options, particularly for a project or business idea, consider the smallest possible risk you can take to test your idea—your 'minimum viable product' to take for a test run and tweak before you invest more heavily in it. Testing a limited set of variables as an experiment can spare you the pain of a more drawn-out failure.

Just remember that failure is an event, not a person. You tried something and didn't get the result you wanted. So what? Don't make it mean any more than that. You are not your failures. So don't be defined by them.

WHEN ANALYSING YOUR FAILURE, DON'T MEASURE YOUR SUCCESS AGAINST THE PLANS YOU HAD WHEN YOU STARTED OUT. MEASURE IT AGAINST THE LESSONS YOU LEARNED WHEN THEY FELL APART.

However big your failure, it serves no-one to spend the rest of your life living in the shadow of a past mistake. Far better is to fail forward: to pick yourself up, extract the greatest possible learning and value you can from the experience and get back on your horse.

FAIL FORWARD

Where have I interpreted failure as an inadequacy on my part, or laid all the blame on others? How has that limited my success?

If I gave myself permission to fail, what would I try doing?

How can I test my idea to ensure that if things don't work as I'd like, I've minimised the possible downside and failed smarter?

First say to yourself
what would you be,
and then do what
you have to do.

EPICTETUS

USE STRESS, DON'T SPREAD IT

When horticulturalists are preparing their plants for life outside the hothouse, they gradually expose them to greater variations of temperature to toughen them up for the variability they will be exposed to in the natural environment. The same principle applies in life. Only by being exposed to situations that put some strain on you – even if that's not always particularly comfortable – can you build your capacity for bigger challenges and perform at your peak.

Conversely, if you're never stretched, over time you lose confidence, resilience and strength. It's why exposure to stress is a vital stimulus for growth. Without it, you can wither on the vine of life.

While life can hold some big challenges, it's the relatively small things that create the most stress in our daily lives. Filing taxes. Family gatherings. Home renovations. Difficult employees. Work deadlines. Minor accidents. Juggling commitments. It's easy to make small problems seem big—stressing about stuff for no other reason than that we've told ourselves 'it's stressful'. Little wonder Richard Carlson sold millions of copies of his book *Don't Sweat the Small Stuff … and it's all small stuff*. It spoke to all those people who find it difficult not to stress about the 'small stuff'.

Of course, stress often gets a bad rap. It's why there's a multibillion-dollar industry built on managing it better. Yet stress itself is not the enemy; it's stressful thinking we need to be careful about. I mean, just think how many times you've heard yourself or others say something like 'My job/client/study/commute/boss/kids/life is so stressful'.

When we say things like this what we're really saying is that we're responding in stressful ways to these people or situations. The irony is that talking about how much stress you feel only makes you feel more stressed and spreads your stress to others. But it doesn't end there. As your internal stress barometer dials up, your ability to cope with other challenges goes down, sending you into a downward 'stress spiral'. All the while, the toll mounts—on you and all those around you. It can be a vicious cycle. (I feel stressed just writing about it!)

The reality is that stress itself is not a medical condition, but a psychological one that triggers physiological responses in your body. In fact, there's a direct link between your stress levels and the story you tell yourself about your ability to handle the demands that you think will be placed on you—real or perceived. It all lies in the interpretation.

FOR BETTER OR WORSE, YOUR PERCEPTION BECOMES YOUR REALITY.

So instead of trying to avoid stress, try putting a new spin on it. One that doesn't leave you a powerless victim but that allows you to choose how you respond to it. As you can see from this simple diagram, your greatest power lies in the space between stimulus and response. Just because there's a lot going on or expected of you there's no need to freak out or fall apart. That's on you.

The truth is that you need stress in your life to get out and do what needs to be done: to play your best game. Just imagine if Novak Djokovic was so chilled out that he napped five minutes before he was due to walk onto centre court at the Australian Open, or if Beyoncé was so chillaxed she needed a reminder that she was performing at the Super Bowl in a few hours' time. Neither of these stars would have ever gotten to where they are without a little stress.

Harnessed well, stress enables you to focus on playing your best game and to thrive in life. It sharpens your concentration and makes you more competitive—particularly when the stakes are high and the slightest edge can make all the difference.

IT'S THEREFORE IMPORTANT TO EMBRACE STRESS AS A VALUABLE FORCE OF LIFE THAT CAN BE EITHER HIGHLY CONSTRUCTIVE OR DESTRUCTIVE, DEPENDING ON HOW YOU MANAGE IT.

The truth is that when we're in the middle of a crisis, most people aren't particularly good at forecasting how they'll feel further down the track. In fact, we tend to project our current stress levels indefinitely into the future and assume we'll always feel as we do now. Called 'negative forecasting bias', it means we tend to underestimate our ability to recover from setbacks and to handle stress. It's not that we aren't hurting or things aren't stressful. It's just that we won't hurt for as long or feel as much stress for as long as we think we will. So no matter how overwhelmed you may feel in the moment, it *will* get better.

As you think about what you have on in your life right now, consider how you can reframe what you're dealing with so that you approach it with a greater sense of belief in your own ability to handle what's coming your way.

You can start by becoming more mindful about what you're feeling in any given moment and staying alert to your own stress responses: clenching fists, biting nails, speaking fast, irritability or plain old distractedness that leads to misplacing your phone or car keys!

Once you've done this, tune in to what you're telling yourself about the stimulus that is triggering your stress. What language are you using to describe what's going on? Instead of saying (to yourself or others) that you're nervous, say you're excited. Instead of saying someone is stressing you out, say they're challenging you. Instead of describing your situation as a disaster or a nightmare, describe it as challenging but manageable. Instead of describing yourself as a basket-case, remind yourself that 'you've got this' (because you have!). The very words you use can dial up your stress and turn you into a basket-case or they can dial it down. It's not the situation that determines which; it's you.

SHIPS DON'T SINK BECAUSE OF THE WATER THAT'S AROUND THEM. THEY SINK BECAUSE OF THE WATER THAT GETS IN THEM. DON'T LET WHAT'S GOING ON AROUND YOU GET INSIDE YOU.

To quote Wayne Dyer, 'There is no stress in the world. Just people having stressful thoughts'. Take responsibility for using stress to serve a positive outcome and for not spreading it to others.

Most things you stress about never actually happen. As I often tell my kids, 'Live the worry once'.

REWORK STRESS

Where has my talking about how stressful things are and feeding off the reaction (sympathy or admiration) from those around me been unhelpful?

Where has feeling a degree of stress been to my advantage in my life up to now?

Think about what is on my plate right now – pressures, problems and problem people. What is another way of describing it that dials down my stress levels and dials up my confidence to handle it all?

I am not afraid of storms for I am learning to sail my ship.

LOUISA MAY ALCOTT

SHED YOUR OLD BAGGAGE

Anger. Hurt. Blame. Shame. Many people walk through each day weighed down with a heavy load of excess baggage they've accumulated from past experiences that cannot be undone. Yet while it's impossible to change past events, you can change the story you tell yourself about them. In doing so, you can leave the emotions you've carried like a ball and chain where they belong.

In the past.

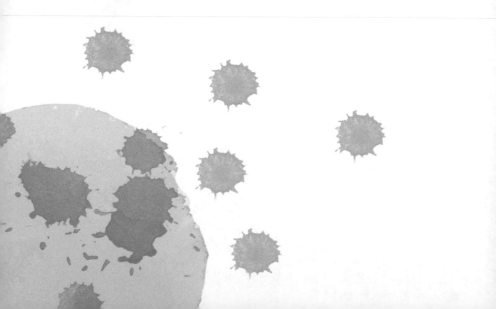

Ernest Hemingway once wrote that life breaks us all, but some of us become stronger in the broken places. Those who become stronger 'in the broken places' are not born stronger. Rather, they become stronger because they decide not to let past experiences determine their future. They leave behind the anger, the guilt, the shame and the blame, and carry forward with them only the lessons they hold.

So too can you.

You, and you alone, get to choose whether something (or someone) that has wounded you in the past will make you more isolated or more connected, more broken or more whole. And while forgiveness—of yourself and others—is a decision you may have to make again and again, it's ultimately your decision whether you bless the past and move on, or harbour it and keep hurting. As Nobel Prize laureate Toni Morrison once said, 'Wanna fly, you got to give up the shit that weighs you down'.

Of course, you don't need a therapist—much less a book—to tell you that negative emotions about a past that cannot be changed will limit your future, which can. You already know that.

The question is, when will you finally decide to let those emotions go and move on? On your death bed? When you get the forgiveness you want, the apology you deserve or the justice you seek? Let's face it, it hasn't come yet so chances are it never will.

YOUR PAST DOES NOT HAVE TO EQUAL YOUR FUTURE… UNLESS YOU LIVE THERE.

If you're okay with carrying hurt, anger, blame and shame from the past into your future, then go right ahead and keep on keeping on. Just be really clear in your own heart that what you're gaining from hanging onto those emotions is worth what you're giving up. Like your ability to feel a deep sense of joy, peace, intimacy and love in the rest of your life. If you're not sure, ask the people you care about most. Just make sure they feel safe enough to tell you the answer.

EXPERIENCE HAS TAUGHT ME THAT WHATEVER ANGER, HURT, BLAME OR SHAME WE ARE HOLDING ONTO FROM THE PAST, WE CARRY INTO EVERY OTHER RELATIONSHIP IN SOME WAY.

Your past may have shaped you, but it doesn't define you and it certainly doesn't have to limit who you can become. That's your call. Entirely. So let's take a look at your excess baggage. Bring to mind any long-term grudges, hurts, guilt, blame or shame. Then reflect on the following questions.

LIGHTEN THE LOAD

What have I gained from holding on to anger, hurt, blame and shame about something that can't be changed?

What is a new story that I can tell myself about what happened that moves me towards healing, hope and wholeness?

Think about a relationship that may have caused you to feel a lot of resentment, heartache or hurt. Then ask yourself:

What would be lifted from me if I decided to forgive that person, regardless of whether they have ever sought my forgiveness?

If you are ready to forgive them, write them a letter (you don't need to send it... just writing it alone can be a powerful execise).

MY HARD-WON WISDOM

When life's storms roll in and your plans fall apart, it matters less what you expect from life than what life expects from you. Within you is everything you need to meet the challenge, beginning with refusing to let it define you.

My mantra for when life doesn't go to plan is ...

I will never again let my mistakes, failures, setbacks or struggles define me because I know ...

The most valuable lesson I've learned from my hardest experiences is ...

Next time I find myself starting to feel stressed I will ...

BUILD YOUR TRIBE

MASTERY OF LIFE IS NOT A SOLO
ENDEAVOUR. WHEN YOU SURROUND
YOURSELF WITH THE PEOPLE WHO BRING
OUT YOUR BEST AND EMBOLDEN YOUR
THINKING, YOU CAN DO MORE, BE MORE
AND GIVE MORE THAN YOU EVER COULD
OTHERWISE. WE ARE BRAVER TOGETHER
THAN WE CAN EVER BE ALONE.

We are innately social beings. As such, we're at our best when we're deeply connected to other people.

But not just to any people. To people who respect our individuality, bring out our best and broaden our thinking.

Perhaps you already have people like that in your life. People who you feel safe to be around—with whom you can lower your guard, expose your vulnerability, confide your struggles, share your dreams and celebrate your wins. People you can count on to have your back, hold your feet to the fire (when your fear rises up) and tell you the truth, even when it's hard to hear. People who help you be a better version of yourself and whom you can trust. Deeply.

While we live in an increasingly individualistic society we need each other every bit as much today as we ever have. Yet recent studies have found that despite being more interconnected than at any time in history, people feel increasingly alone. Surprisingly, those who report feeling loneliest are those you'd expect it from least: those under 35, who are the most prolific social networkers of all.

Social media appeals to our vulnerability and vanity, yet it also provides the illusion of friendship which, in real life, can be superficial and is unable to meet our deeper need for truly intimate friendships. Whereas only a few decades ago, in the pre-Facebook era, most people reported having four or five close friends to whom they could say anything, today most only have two or three, and the number of people who report having no close confidants has doubled.

While it might be stating the obvious, if you want to *connect* with people more, you need to *converse* with people more—openly, authentically and with a vulnerability that may sometimes feel uncomfortable.

IT'S WHY BUILDING YOUR TRIBE ISN'T ABOUT QUANTITY, IT'S ABOUT QUALITY.

The people you surround yourself with either raise or lower your expectations; shrink or expand your aspirations; broaden or narrow your thinking. They will help to realise your brilliance or keep you from ever knowing it.

Since every interaction you have with another human being involves an exchange of energy—positive or negative—your relationships are magnifiers of emotions, for better or worse. You'll have already experienced this from the times you've spent with negative people, perhaps more aptly called 'emotional vampires'. They leave you feeling drained of energy and if you're exposed to their pessimism or anxiety often enough, eventually it starts wearing off on you.

The flipside is also true: spending time with 'energy givers'—people who are big hearted, optimistic and passionate about life—will help you become more that way yourself.

SURROUNDING YOURSELF WITH A COMMUNITY OF PEOPLE WHO BRING OUT YOUR BEST AND EMBOLDEN YOUR VISION EMPOWERS YOU TO MAKE THE DIFFERENCE YOUR DIFFERENCE MAKES.

Which begs the question:

Whose orbit are you spinning in and who is spinning in yours?

Central to finding your tribe is taking full responsibility for the energy you radiate outwards, because how you 'show up' in the world will affect who 'shows up' in yours.

Constantly complaining won't attract go-getters. Forever worrying what everyone thinks of you won't attract free spirts. Being frugal with your money and tight with your time won't attract big-hearted people who live from abundance—or it might, but they won't hang around for long.

However, if you're committed to speaking truthfully and living authentically, you will attract great people and build the deeply rich and rewarding relationships that make life richer … and more fun! Without truth and authenticity, no relationship worth its salt can stand the test of time.

Of course, as you go through life and move towards whatever it is that lights you up, you can sometimes outgrow your relationships. That doesn't mean you don't care about the people you've shared a season of your life with. Perhaps many. It simply means that continuing to spend a lot of time with them no longer serves you…or them (though they may not see it that way). This isn't disloyal or unkind. It simply reflects your own personal evolution and the reality that some people simply aren't growing in the same direction or at the same pace as you.

YOUR ENERGY IS PRECIOUS. YOU HAVE TO TAKE 100 PER CENT RESPONSIBILITY FOR BOTH THE ENERGY YOU LET INTO YOUR SPACE AS WELL AS THE ENERGY YOU PROJECT OUT.

If the people in your tribe right now aren't pulling for you, maybe it's time you moved on to create space for people who will. Which is what step 6 is all about: helping you find your tribe and build the rewarding relationships that fill your deepest needs and empower you to blaze your brightest trail on your adventure through life.

That doesn't mean all your relationships will be perfect. None are. It *does* mean that you will be *intentional* about who you invest time with, *real* in how you show up for them, and *committed* to having the brave conversations that are the foundation of all meaningful relationships.

IN THE END, YOU CHANGE YOUR TRIBE AND YOUR TRIBE CHANGES YOU.

Either way, make sure it's for the better.

To change one's life,
start immediately,
do it flamboyantly,
no exceptions.

WILLIAM JAMES

BACK YOURSELF, BE YOURSELF

A magnetised piece of iron will lift about 12 times its own weight; yet if it is demagnetised, the same piece of iron can't even lift a feather. Like attracts like. Accordingly, people who radiate passion for life attract opportunities, lucky breaks and passionate people into their lives. The same is true in reverse. Your vibe attracts your tribe.

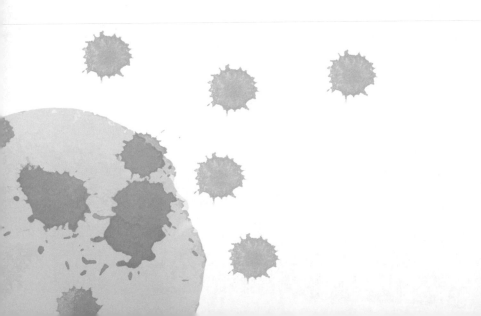

To attract the people and opportunities you want, you need to own yourself, back yourself and be yourself. And when fear gets the better of you, you need to own that too.

THE WONDERFUL IRONY OF SIMPLY BEING YOURSELF IS THAT THE LESS YOU CARE ABOUT WHAT PEOPLE THINK OF YOU, THE MORE THEY ACTUALLY DO.

Likewise, the people you admire the most are those who are least hungry for it. Simply being who you are begins with embracing this truth:

You are innately worthy, imperfectly whole and wholly imperfect.

Period.

While there are people like you, no-one is the same as you. (Which, let's be honest here, isn't such a bad thing—right?) So, for all the pressure you may feel to prove yourself, to impress people or to fit in, it's by owning yourself—and all that makes you different (your own special blend of weird and wonderful)—that will attract to you the people who can help you to become the fullest version of yourself; to be someone people will want to know.

Not *all* people, but the *right* people for you!

THE WORLD IS HUNGRY FOR PEOPLE TO OWN THE DIFFERENCE THEIR DIFFERENCE MAKES. AFTER ALL, WHEN ALL YOU DO IS TRY TO FIT IN AND CONFORM, ALL YOU OFFER IS CONFORMITY.

So doubt yourself less, back yourself more and dim your light for no-one.

As your light gets brighter, you will illuminate the light in others. What greater gift is there?

PROVE YOURSELF TO NO-ONE

Who would I be if I were 100 per cent myself? What parts of myself that sometimes get dialled down (or totally hidden) would find expression in the world?

If I didn't feel the need to prove myself or pretend to be anyone else other than who I am, what would I do more of? What would I do less of?

Where have I been selling myself short? How has that cost me?

The beginning is always today.

MARY WOLLSTONECRAFT

ENLIST YOUR CHEER SQUAD

When you're surrounded by people who are committed to your success (however you define it!), it creates an environment that enables you to do more, go further and bounce back faster than you ever would otherwise.

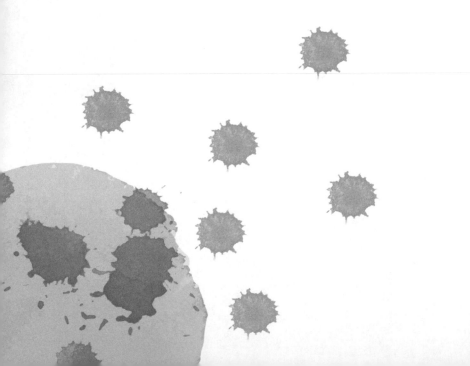

Your vibe attracts your tribe. To attract people who are positive and proactive in their own lives, you need to be positive and proactive in your own.

While big-thinking, braver hearted people may serendipitously walk into your life, you need to do your bit. Find out where the kind of people you want to hang out with hang out themselves and go there. Join a club or group of people who share a common interest, attend a networking event (however awkward you find them!), sign up for a trip, go to a conference or engage in online forums—the more time you spend in places where conversations are occurring about the things that matter to you, the more people you'll meet who will matter also.

There is a caveat here.

Sometimes you'll meet people who feel threatened by you. People who may actually not want you to move forward. If you've known them a while it may be that the courage beneath your choices makes them feel insecure about their own. Or maybe they're afraid you'll leave them behind. Or maybe they're just jealous (but too proud to admit it!).

Live bigger anyway.

Downplaying your achievements and downsizing your goals to not intimidate people doesn't serve anyone. You will never be able to appease those people who measure their own worth based on the success of others.

The greatest service you can do for anyone is to give the best you have to life. But if you can't share your 'wins' with the people in your life because you sense they don't care or won't be delighted to celebrate them with you, then you need to find people who will.

WHATEVER YOU DO, NEVER DIAL YOURSELF DOWN TO LIFT OTHERS UP. IT JUST MAKES EVERYONE SMALLER.

When you dare to be the fullest, most authentic version of who you were born to become, the right people will show up in your life to spin in your orbit.

SURROUND YOURSELF WITH PEOPLE WHO BRING OUT YOUR BEST

If I could recruit my ultimate cheer squad, who would be in it?

What do I value the most about these people?

Who do I know (or know of) that shares these values and I could connect with, engage as a mentor, or enrol into my support network, whether formally or informally?

Are there any people I need to move away from because, despite how long I may have known them, they don't support me and may actually be a source of discouragement? How will it cost me if I do nothing?

What you think
you create, what
you feel you attract,
what you imagine
you become.

··

BUDDHA

LIFT AS YOU CLIMB

You shape your tribe as your tribe shapes you. Be someone who lifts people up and brings out the best in those around you. Someone who helps others think bigger, aim higher and go further than they otherwise would. Someone who sees the spark that others have forgotten, who affirms their values, challenges their stories and always leaves them feeling a little bit bigger and better and braver than they were before.

We grow muscles lifting weights — we grow powerful lifting each other.

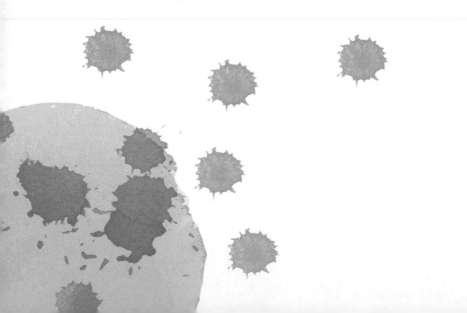

Your family. Your tribe. Your peeps. Your team. Your clan. Your band. Your squad. Your community. Your kin. Your personal board of directors.

It doesn't matter what you call the people you care about most and want on your side as you go through life. All that matters is that you're better off for circling in their orbit and they're better off for circling in yours.

Of course, every relationship is a little give-and-take. Sometimes you receive more from someone than you could ever repay. Accepting help from people can sometimes be uncomfortable, particularly if you feel guilty about being needy or embarrassed about your inability to return the favour. Accept it anyway. The vast majority of people genuinely love to help other people where they can and when you don't accept their offer, you not only deprive yourself of their assistance, you deprive them of the joy they get from giving it. Everyone misses out.

Likewise, there will be times when you have the opportunity to help others in ways that you'd never expect them to reciprocate. Give generously. Not because it's just the right thing to do, but because each time you lift someone up—to be more, to do more, to dare more—you raise yourself and everyone else around you. Not always directly. Not always immediately. Not always obviously. But every act of kindness, of generosity and of service sets in motion a ripple effect whose impact can flow across generations.

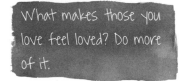
What makes those you love feel loved? Do more of it.

While you can get more done in a day if you're operating alone, over the course of your lifetime you can accomplish far more when you're pulling in the same direction as others. To quote an African proverb: 'If you want to go fast, go alone. If you want to go far, go together'.

NEVER UNDERESTIMATE THE IMPACT *YOU* HAVE ON THOSE AROUND YOU. NOT YOUR WORDS. NOT YOUR ACTIONS. NOT YOUR PRESENCE. NOT YOUR POWER.

If every single day you decided to encourage someone you may not have thought to encourage otherwise, over the course of your life you would profoundly impact thousands of lives in ways beyond anything you could even dare imagine.

LIFT OTHERS AS YOU CLIMB

What do people value most about knowing me?

How can I be that way more often for them?

What is just one thing I can do today to help someone I know ... or someone I don't?

SPEAK FROM THE HEART

We avoid tough conversations for the same reason we don't do so many things that would serve us—it's uncomfortable, it's risky and it's just easier to do nothing. In the short term.

Yet the price we pay for avoiding difficult conversations far exceeds the discomfort we feel in having them. It's why finding the courage to speak from the heart always leaves everyone better off.

Since no two human beings can ever see, think, feel and act exactly the same way on a permanent basis, no relationship is immune to conflict. It's inevitable that over time we will find ourselves frustrated, hurt, disappointed or resentful with other people. Even those we love and admire the most.

YET IT'S NOT THE ISSUES THAT ARISE WHICH CAUSE THE PROBLEMS IN OUR RELATIONSHIPS. IT'S HOW WE DEAL WITH THEM.

The issues that can drive wedges into our relationships expose us to a whole raft of emotions we'd prefer to avoid. Vulnerability. Rejection. Hurt. Embarrassment. Anger. Fear. Sadness. Jealousy. Humiliation. Guilt. Shame. It's why, in the short term at least, it can feel safer and easier to say nothing. Many do.

ISSUES THAT AREN'T TALKED OUT GET ACTED OUT.

When we fail to speak up about what weighs us down, untended emotions bury down and they fester. Left long enough, they ultimately boil back up to the surface where they are expressed in counterproductive ways: in the 'silent treatment', withholding affection and other acts of passive aggression, snide remarks, innuendos, shutting people down, pushing them away or walking away ourselves. Our lack of courage to lay what we're feeling on the table at the outset ultimately damages trust and drives deep wedges into the space once occupied by trust, respect, collaboration, intimacy and affection.

THE QUALITY OF YOUR RELATIONSHIPS IS DETERMINED BY THE QUALITY OF THE CONVERSATIONS YOU HAVE IN THEM. WHEN YOU LET FEAR STOP YOU FROM SAYING WHAT NEEDS TO BE HEARD, YOU BECOME COMPLICIT IN THE BREAKDOWN OF TRUST IN THE RELATIONSHIP.

The word 'courage' comes from the Latin cor, for 'heart'. It's why we can only speak courageously when we are living wholeheartedly. After all, what comes from the heart, will land on the heart. It explains why we connect more deeply with people when we're sharing our vulnerabilities than when we're sharing our victories. If you've ever known someone who only talks about their wins and how together they are, you'll know this already.

Likewise, when you enter into an emotionally sensitive conversation with the genuine desire to make things better for everyone (not just to prove yourself right, make others wrong or pull them down a peg or two), your relationships are always better off. So if there's something you genuinely want to say, the odds are that someone genuinely needs to hear it and that you'll all be better off saying it.

As illustrated by the following diagram, the quality of the conversations you have lay the foundation for the results you create in your life. Speaking truth with kindness builds relationships, which grows trust, expanding influence and leading to actions that create outcomes. Yet it all begins with having the courage to say what needs to be said … with less fear, pride, arrogance and ego.

This is as true in your close personal relationships as it is in your workplace, your children's school, your local community … your country and at peace-making tables around the world! Never has the world needed more people in power to speak truth with kindness — not to make their own lives better, but to leave everyone better off.

SPEAK BRAVELY

What have I learned from the times in the past when I've put off a difficult conversation?

How can I apply that learning to an issue that has the potential to create a wedge in some relationships right now?

What is something I genuinely need to say to someone right now? How will it cost me if I don't?

ENLIST PEOPLE IN YOUR CAUSE

The more people who know what you want, the more who can help you get it. Yet most of us were brought up to believe that asking for help is a sign of weakness: a last resort for desperate times. In fact, it's just the opposite.

Asking for help shows that you are brave enough to admit you can't do it all alone. It doesn't mean you're weak; it means you want to be stronger.

Think of something that's been annoying you, causing you to feel resentful, frustrated or undervalued in some way. Got it? Now consider if there's a request that you could have been making of people—something you could have asked for, but haven't.

Having held back from reaching out for support over the years for fear of seeming needy, being rejected or just putting people out—only to regret it later—I've learned an important lesson. It's this:

ASKING FOR WHAT YOU WANT CORRELATES VERY HIGHLY WITH GETTING IT.

Assuming that people should just know what you want is a recipe for frustration, disappointment, regret and resentment. If you've been feeling any of that, then it's a sure sign that there's a request that you could be making that you haven't made.

So whether it's getting support to achieve a goal, return to school, start a business, close one down, lose that weight, land that promotion, find your soulmate, fund a venture or exit a job you loathe so you can find one you love, having the courage to enlist support from others can make all the difference.

Not only that, but when you ask people to help you, you give them the opportunity to practise generosity, which sometimes serves the giver even more than the receiver. What a shame it would be to let your fear of being rejected or appearing needy deprive them of that. After all, this is not just about elevating yourself. It's about elevating everyone.

GIVE PEOPLE THE OPPORTUNITY TO HELP YOU

Who can help me move towards achieving something I want or changing something I don't?

What would I like to ask of them? (*Be as specific as you can.*)

What am I potentially leaving on the table by not asking?

When can I talk to them? (*Find a time. Set it up. Make it happen.*)

MY TRIBAL TREATY

The kind of people I will surround myself with are people who ...
(*The values, traits and beliefs you write down should reflect those you want to embody yourself.*)

My vibe attracts my tribe. To attract and build the rich relationships I want I will be ...

To encourage others to live bigger, braver lives I am committed to ...

Set your life on
fire. Seek those who
fan your flames.

RUMI

RUN YOUR OWN BEST RACE

TRUE SUCCESS ISN'T A DESTINATION; IT'S A FEELING. IT FLOWS FROM FORGIVING YOUR FALLIBILITY, CELEBRATING YOUR BLESSINGS AND FOCUSING ON DOING THE BEST YOU CAN WITH WHAT YOU HAVE. GENUINE SUCCESS IS NOT DETERMINED BY YOUR EXPERIENCES *IN* LIFE, BUT BY YOUR CAPACITY *FOR* LIFE. BUILD IT DAILY.

This book began by inviting you to connect with the highest vision for your life...to decide what you want your life to stand for...to find your 'why'.

Which is all well and good. But the biggest challenge many of us face as we juggle life's priorities and pressures is to live our 'why' on a daily basis. To show up for life purposefully, passionately and fully present...day in, day out.

Easier said than done, right?

Which is what running your own best race is all about.

To help you bring your best self to your biggest challenges...daily.

On the days when everything goes marvellously to plan and on the days when nothing does. On the days you're well rested and ready to take on the world and on the days when you're tired from being up all night with the kids and you want to sack your clients.

THE REALITY IS THAT IF IT WERE EASY TO BRING YOUR BEST SELF TO THE BIG GAME OF LIFE EVERY DAY YOU'D BE DOING IT ALREADY.

But it's not.

You're busy. You're juggling. You feel constantly pulled in different directions, you aren't sure where to focus first and while you understand intellectually that your experience of life is up to you, you sometimes find it hard, like *really* hard, to 'hug the curves' and channel your inner Braveheart. Don't even mention trying to 'lift as you climb!' Heck, how can anyone think of climbing when they just want a nap!

Rest assured, you don't struggle alone.

While some people may wake up in the morning ready to take on the world, many wake up with no grander intention than not dropping anything that's already on their plate.

It's why you need to set yourself up for success. *Daily*. Doing whatever it takes to put your best foot forward. *Daily*. And on those days when you lose it at your kids or spouse—when you drop the ball or just want to throttle someone with it—forgiving your fallibility, picking your sorry self back up and moving on…a little more humble, but no less whole, than before.

Just as a car that gets a regular tune-up goes further on less fuel, travels better over bumps and hugs the curves better, so too will you go further, stress less and handle life's twists and turns better when you've taken time out to 'tune up'—body, mind and spirit.

IRONICALLY ENOUGH, IT'S NOT THE BIG THINGS YOU DO EVERY ONCE IN A WHILE – THE ANNUAL VACATION, SPA RETREAT OR WEEKEND AWAY – THAT HAVE THE BIGGEST IMPACT ON HOW YOU SHOW UP FOR LIFE. IT'S THE SMALL THINGS YOU DO EACH DAY – THE ONES FEW MAY SEE – WHICH PRODUCE THE BIG RESULTS THAT EVERYONE WANTS.

So get ready to invest more time in the small things that will help you do everything else better!

EXPAND YOUR CAPACITY FOR LIFE

Energy is the basic building block of life. Without it, you can't get out of bed each morning, much less bring passion to life or persevere with your challenges. Investing time each day to recharge your energy, refocus your mind and refuel your spirit will enable you to show up more powerfully and be a source of positivity for all who enter your orbit.

Many people complain that they just don't have time to get everything they want to get done in a day. Yet the truth is that most of us run out of energy long before we run out of time.

As you can see in the energy matrix below, there are different types of energy and they can have a profoundly different impact on our lives. High energy, low energy. Positive energy, negative energy. While there are times we all find ourselves feeling negative energy, if we spend too much time in the emotions that embody it, they form a dark cloud that taints every experience and makes life pretty bleak.

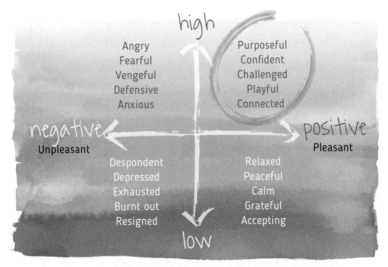

The Energy Matrix (modified from the work of Jim Loehr and Tony Schwartz)

Learning how to manage and shift your energy is pivotal to thriving in life and making the most of your circumstances, particularly those that can pull you down. As Jim Loehr and Tony Schwartz wrote in *The Power of Full Engagement*, 'Because energy capacity diminishes both with overuse and underuse, we must balance energy expenditure with intermittent energy renewal'.

The challenge is spending most of your time in the right-hand quadrants, moving between low- and high-positive energy. Low-positive energy is beneficial in refuelling your battery and reconnecting to purpose, but it's when we're operating from high-positive energy that we get stuff done! The question is, what will it take for you to spend more time in the top right quadrant?

While there are thousands of great books on how to have more energy, you probably already know things you can do to lift your energy that you just aren't doing (or not doing enough of). So before we get into specifics, consider that optimal energy is the result of an alignment with each of the core dimensions:

- *Physical*—stamina, vitality and an overall sense of wellbeing. Physical energy lies at the foundation of all other energy.

- *Mental*—clear focus on your top priorities; flexible and open to changing course

- *Emotional*—a sense of belonging, self-confidence, optimism and resilience

- *Spiritual*—alignment with your deepest values and connection to a purpose bigger than yourself

Whenever something is out of alignment in any of these domains, your energy is compromised.

While life will sometimes land you in circumstances that require a lot of energy just to make it through, you always have to take full responsibility for the activities and rituals you embed in your daily life that restore and amplify your energy.

spiritual
LIVE FROM 'WHY'

emotional
NURTURE GRACE AND GRIT

mental
PUT FIRST THINGS FIRST

physical
EAT WELL, SLEEP ENOUGH, MOVE OFTEN

BUILD THE RITUALS FOR YOUR BEST LIFE
Physical

I am at my best physically when I feel... (*Energetic? Rested? Strong? Fit? In shape? A sense of vitality?*)

To feel this way more often I will... (*List daily rituals, habits and actions you can take, such as what you will eat to fuel your body, scheduling exercise and other activities to optimise immune health, manage stress, and enhance stamina and wellbeing.*)

Mental

I am at my best mentally when I feel ... (*Focused? I'm working from my strengths? Clear-headed? Flexible? Unstoppable?*)

To feel this way more often I will... (*List here what you can do to stay focused and work from your strengths. For instance, 90-day goal review sessions, setting up time-management systems, daily planning, blocking 'thinking' time into your schedule, working out, meditation.*)

Emotional

I am at my best emotionally when I feel ... (*Supported? Connected? Compassionate? Confident? Brave? Resilient? Playful? Optimistic?*)

To feel this way more often I will ... (*List daily rituals, habits and actions you can take to re-centre and restore yourself, such as spending time in nature, exercising, connecting with your tribe and hobbies.*)

Spiritual

I am at my best spiritually when I feel... *(Aligned? Purposeful? Forgiving?)*

To feel this way more often I will... *(List daily rituals, habits and actions you can take, such as journalling, praying, yoga, reading inspirational literature and meditating.)*

TAKE NOTHING FOR GRANTED

How many of the things you once dreamed of – finding your partner for life, your children, your salary, the home you live in or the car you drive – have gradually become the norm?

Gratitude takes effort. Yet making gratitude a regular practice pays a steep dividend. After all, it's not happy people who are the most grateful; it's grateful people who are the most happy.

After 10 sand-blasted days crossing the Sahara desert through Algeria, I arrived in the town of Agadez in northern Niger. After a long-awaited shower (albeit a cold one), I went for a walk through the market, where I met some men from the local Hausa tribe. When they invited me to drink tea with them, I immediately accepted. I received a royal welcome into their humble abode and as I sat on the floor with them sipping sweet tea, their children playing in the red dirt outside, I was struck by how thankful they were to have me as their guest. Almost too thankful. After all, here I was with the means to be travelling in a place far from my home and they didn't even own a chair for me to sit on.

It was many years later that I happened to tune into a radio interview with someone from the Hausa tribe. As he talked about the importance of gratitude in their culture, he shared an old Hausa saying: *It is when we're thankful for a little, we get a lot.* It was then that it struck me that the men I had met years earlier had embodied the essence of this saying. They may have lacked worldly riches, but they radiated a wealth of life.

I'm sure that you, like me, have met people who many might say landed the 'jackpot' in life, yet who seem perpetually dissatisfied and always wanting for more. But no matter what more they get, it is never enough. We can all fall into the same trap.

THE TRUTH IS THAT GRATITUDE HAS NOTHING TO DO WITH GOOD FORTUNE.

Unleashing the power of gratitude power in your daily life therefore takes no more than recognising that life itself is a gift, that it has an expiry date and that every day can be lifted by simply focusing on all you have to be grateful for. If you have money in the bank and change in your wallet you are in the 8 per cent of the world's most wealthy.

If you go to bed tonight with more health than illness, you are more blessed than the million people who will die this week. If you have never experienced the terror of war or the pangs of starvation, you are luckier than 500 million people who have. And if you are reading this now, then you are more fortunate than 3 billion people in the world who never had the opportunity to learn to read.

> Gratitude is a tonic for life's difficulties, a magnifier of its blessings and indispensable for happiness.

Tony Robbins has said that when we're grateful, fear disappears and abundance appears. It's why gratitude is the single most powerful virtue we can practise if we're to be fully present to the gift of life and all the blessings that fill it. Not just the big things, but the little things. In fact the little things most of all. Because one day you will look back and realise that it was all those little things that were actually the big things.

Each time you practise gratitude you sow the seed for more blessings to grow in your life. But even more important, each time you practise gratitude you become more of a blessing for others. Therein lies the real gold.

SOW GRATITUDE

What are 20 things I'm grateful for right now?

What is a difficult event from my life which, at the time, felt like anything but a blessing? Write it down and then reflect on what you gained from the experience that helped you become the person you are today, including how you can use it as a gift for those around you.

OWN YOUR 'ENOUGHNESS'

We live in a culture that celebrates perfectionism even as it censures it. One that is constantly pressuring us to live up to some idealised image of beauty or brilliance, or both.

So many of us spend our entire lives trying to smooth out our rough edges and shore up our shortcomings in our effort to become the person we most want to be – the person we think we should be. Yet no matter how hard we try, we still don't feel we're enough.

It's why living your best life and making your fullest mark on the world doesn't require you being perfect – it requires you to have the courage to be nothing more and no-one else but your flawsomely awesome and imperfectly adequate self.

You are fabulous and fallible, brilliant and blundering, innately loveable and wholly imperfect. You are one big, glorious fusion of dark and light, of all that is good and of all that isn't.

And that's okay.

WHEN YOU EMBRACE YOUR OWN FALLIBILITY, OWN YOUR QUIRKS AND ACCEPT YOUR FAULTS, YOU DON'T LOWER THE BAR AND RELEASE YOUR DEMONS; YOU BRING THEM OUT OF THE SHADOW AND ACCENTUATE YOUR LIGHT.

Yet even the most enlightened among us would tell you that doing that is a lifelong endeavour with no finish line. Which is also okay. Really.

Because whatever bright spark came up with the term 'human *beings*' got it wrong. A far better term would have been 'human *becomings*' since, let's face it, we're a work in progress.

No matter how hard we try, we'll always slip up, fall down and fail to be all we think we should be: boundlessly brave, perpetually passionate, unconditionally loving and unfailingly tolerant.

Like, daily.

Sometimes hourly (or maybe that's just me).

And despite intellectually understanding that we're not perfect, we still use our lack of perfection as a baton to beat ourselves up. (If you're a woman, double it. If you're a mother, double it again!)

I *AM* ENOUGH. I *ALWAYS HAVE BEEN* ENOUGH. I *ALWAYS WILL BE* ENOUGH.

Just imagine if you could live every day of the rest of your life with that belief. Seriously.

Just imagine, if every single day you stepped out into the world with the deep knowing that you don't have to be more or less of anything in order to be enough — to be loveable enough, good enough, smart enough, worthy enough.

Just imagine if you owned your innate 'enoughness'!

WHAT IF, INSTEAD OF CONTINUALLY STRIVING TO BE THE PERSON YOU THINK YOU SHOULD BE, YOU EMBRACED THE MARVELLOUSNESS OF THE PERSON YOU ALREADY ARE?

And what if you tried, however imperfectly, to celebrate the fact that you are truly magnificent, *at this very moment*, for all that you are and for all that you're not, for all that you've done and for all that you haven't?

Because, despite how quickly you may be able to reel off your shortcomings (I'm sure your list is no longer than mine), it is the parts of you that you'd rather keep tucked away out of sight that actually help you to accentuate the light.

Given this truth (because, take it from me, it is the truth), where do you need to stop waiting until you are perfect before you'll give yourself permission to embrace the spirit that's been burning inside you your entire life? And where do you need to stop waiting to do something perfectly before you give yourself permission to strike out?

PERFECTIONISM IS THE ENEMY OF SELF-EXPRESSION, CREATION AND CONTRIBUTION. IT STANDS BETWEEN YOU AND WHAT YOU YEARN FOR MOST.

Becoming the fullest version of the imperfect 'human ~~being~~ becoming' you have it within you to be will only happen when you embrace that truth and step forward anyway.

Life's perfection exists in its imperfection and your greatest work won't come from the parts of you that are flawless; it will come from the parts of you that you've been wrestling with your entire life. The rough and raw parts that make you real, that make you relatable and from which you forge the most meaningful connections with others (I mean, who wants to hang out with a perfect person!).

In *The Gifts of Imperfection*, Brené Brown wrote that 'Perfectionism never happens in a vacuum. It touches everyone around you'. The flipside of this is that when you own your imperfection and choose to shine your brightest anyway, you give others permission to do the same. What greater gift is there?

EMBRACE YOURSELF AS A HUMAN ~~BEING~~ BECOMING

Where do I need to forgive myself for not being perfect?

How could giving my permission to be imperfect free me up to *do* more, *dare* more and *give* more?

If I owned my 'enoughness' and fully accepted myself as a human ~~being~~ becoming, how would that liberate me to experience greater joy, gratitude, connection and intimacy?

How does getting off my own back expand my capacity to be kinder with others, more forgiving and less judgemental?

DITCH COMPARISONS

You wouldn't be human if you didn't occasionally find yourself peeking over the fence and comparing your lot with those around you. Particularly the people with whom you share a common background or interest. Family members. Work colleagues. Competitors. Old friends. Neighbours.

While comparing can sometimes leave you grateful, more often it sets you at war with yourself, leaving you feeling like you're falling behind on some measure. Let others run their own race. Focus on yours only.

Let's face it, the world thrives on diversity. It needs the full spectrum of talents, strengths, passions and personalities. Yet too often we fall into the trap of wishing we were more like other people and less like ourselves. 'Then I'd be more successful,' we tell ourselves. 'Then I'd be happier, more valued, more influential…'.

It's a lie.

We each have our own special mark to make and it would be a pretty boring world if we were all making the same one. The hard truth is that you don't need to be more like anyone else—nor would the world be better off if you were.

Do some people seem to have that Midas touch and get on a lucky streak that never ends? Sure. Some people do *seem* to do that. But then that's because we tend to compare others' strengths to our weaknesses and their outsides to our insides. We make assumptions about their life based only on what we can glimpse of it, when in reality we have no idea what they've had to do or give up to get to where they are. Nor do we know what they are privately wrestling with right now.

EVERY ONE OF US HAS OUR OWN MOUNTAINS TO CLIMB, OUR OWN FEARS TO CONQUER, OUR OWN HEARTACHES TO HEAL AND OUR OWN OPPORTUNITIES TO SEIZE.

Spending time looking over at what others are doing may be natural, but what everyone else is doing (earning, making, saying, learning, losing and living in) is irrelevant beyond the invitation it extends for you to cultivate compassion, exercise gratitude and avoid their mistakes.

The truth is that every minute you spend comparing how well you're doing against anyone else is a minute you aren't spending doing better yourself.

You will create more of the good luck you sometimes envy in others when you stay focused on making the very most of what's right in front of you—and *within* you—rather than looking across to see whether you're gaining or, God forbid, losing ground on those around you.

It's why for you to live your own best life—to show up fully and live authentically—you have to run your own best race. Not the race your brother is running, or your best friend or anyone else you compare yourself to.

Your. Own. Best. Race.

While you may sometimes find your eyes glancing out of your lane to see what others are up to in theirs, you can only ever truly 'win' at life when you focus on making the most you can with what you've got. In Wayne Dyer's words, 'True nobility isn't about being better than anyone else. It's about being better than you used to be'.

SO WASTE NO MORE TIME ENVYING THE GIFTS OR GOOD LUCK OF OTHERS. FOCUS ON ONE THING ONLY: MAKING THE MOST OF YOUR OWN.

When you give up comparing, you win.

RUN YOUR OWN RACE

Where has comparing my 'lot' with others' left me feeling 'less than' in some way?

What would I start doing if I stopped envying the gifts and good luck of others and instead started focusing only on making the most of my own?

TRUST YOUR INNER SAGE

Intuition. Gut instinct. Sixth sense. Higher power. Divine guidance. God.

Sometimes it speaks to you as a gentle inkling. Other times it is a weird hunch, a general sense of foreboding or an inexplicable knowing. At *all* times it is nudging you to pay attention to something, or someone; to steer in a particular direction. One that often defies rational analysis and transcends pure logic but that always serves your highest good.

That little voice has your back. Trust it.

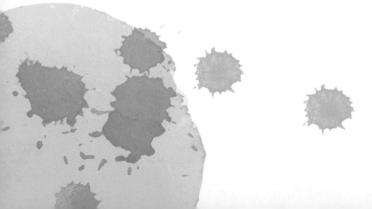

French philosopher and Jesuit priest Pierre Teilhard de Chardin once said that 'we are not physical beings having a spiritual experience; we are spiritual beings having a physical experience'.

People with a sense of the spiritual dimension of life find this easy to accept. Others less so. Whatever your religious or spiritual beliefs, or lack thereof, your 'inner knowing' can be your most powerful guide as you navigate your own best path through the dangers and opportunities, and the twists and turns of life.

As I wrote in *Brave*, tuning in to your intuition takes courage. Courage to put aside your spreadsheets, stop re-running the numbers and to trust in something that defies pure reason to guide you forward. Yet if you've ever ignored a hunch or gone against that gut instinct, you'll already know that ignoring your own inner GPS can be costly.

So if you're cynical about the power of your intuition, try this little experiment. Take a couple of deep breaths, close your eyes and visualise holding in your heart something you've been wrestling with. Over the next few days, stay alert for those gentle nudges and subtle (or maybe not-so-subtle) messages from the universe. Don't judge them, don't resist them. Just trust that the wisest part of you is looking out for you. Because it is.

All faith is an experiment but you can't get the results if you don't do the experiments.

It would be nice if you did your bit to help it along.

ALBERT EINSTEIN SPOKE OF INTUITION AS A SACRED GIFT AND LIKENED RATIONALITY TO A FAITHFUL SERVANT. IN OUR CULTURE OF SCIENTIFIC PROOF AND CLINICAL VERIFICATION, WE MUST BE CAREFUL NOT TO IDOLISE ONLY THE RATIONAL AND IGNORE THE SACRED.

As 'spiritual beings' we must lean in to the unknowable, the mystical, the spiritual, and trust the source from which we have come to steer us in the right direction … onto whatever path we're here to walk.

CHANNEL YOUR WISEST SELF

Take five deep breaths, right down into the pit of your belly. Breathe in faith, breathe out fear. Then, as you get really quiet, ask yourself this question and let your pen flow in whatever direction it pleases.

What does the wisest part of me want me to know right now?

The aim, if reached or not, makes great the life.

ROBERT BROWNING

PRIORITISE WHAT TRULY MATTERS

More and more today, people pride themselves on being busy. Very busy. So busy in fact that they don't have time to ask themselves the simple question: Busy for the sake of what?

While our busyness can bolster our sense of significance (as though somehow the busier we are the more important we must be), it can also distract us from the real business of life – of doing the best we can with what we have.

Far better than being proud of your busyness is being proud of the mark you're making – the family you're raising, the value you're adding and the person you're being.

I know that you, like me and most other people you know, are busy. Very busy. Then again, who isn't? Yet there's a distinct difference between being busy and being productive; between being efficient and being effective; between cramming activity into life and living a life that matters.

People who haven't taken the time to clarify what they most want to achieve can easily find themselves spinning lots of plates ... with one arm tied behind their back ... blindfolded ... yet falling short of showing up fully, purposefully, for life.

It's why running your best race requires continually asking yourself whether what you're committing to aligns with the big vision you are most committed to.

A LACK OF CLARITY ABOUT YOUR HIGHEST PRIORITIES CAN LEAVE YOU MAJORING IN MINORING; MOVING FAST BUT LIVING SHALLOW; FURIOUSLY SPINNING PLATES TO MUCH APPLAUSE, BUT DEPRIVING YOURSELF AND THE WORLD OF THE MARK YOU MIGHT OTHERWISE MAKE.

It's why taking time out from your busyness to create, and then regularly revisit, your highest priorities—your very own 'Hell Yes!' list—is always time well spent. Doing this gives you clarity to know how to schedule your time and courage to say a gracious and guilt-free 'no' to the things you may otherwise have taken on for fear of causing disappointment or offence, or of missing out. After all, every time you say 'yes' to one thing you are, by default, saying 'no' to something else.

So if you cannot say a big, loud 'Hell Yes!' to what you're doing, and put your heart into it, then do yourself a favour and take yourself out of it. Doing something that isn't aligned with your highest calling does everyone a disservice. You most of all!

Of course, there's a reason people spend a lot of time racing from one thing to the next yet failing to accomplish anything near what they're capable of. Their constant activity fills a need for significance, yet requires putting little on the line.

You need to be brutally honest about the price you are paying—personally and professionally—when you allow the 'trivial many' to crowd out your days and keep you from focusing on your 'vital few'. Doing this will provide 'push motivation' to move you towards more of what you want in your life (like more vitality, connection, creativity or contentment) and 'pull motivation' to move you away from what you want less of (like stress, frustration, resentment, isolation, exhaustion, procrastination and overwhelm).

LIFE IS FOUND IN THE DANCE BETWEEN WHAT YOU DESIRE MOST AND WHAT YOU FEAR MOST.

As you engage in the dance, you must expect that sometimes your fears will outstep your desires. Such is being human. Yet it is by choosing growth over comfort, purpose over pride and service over safety that you will regain your footing and make your mark.

Teddy Roosevelt once said, 'Far better it is to dare mighty things, to win glorious triumphs, even though checkered by failure, than to rank with those poor spirits who neither enjoy nor suffer much, because they live in the gray twilight that knows not victory nor defeat'.

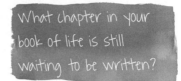

SOMETIMES YOU HAVE TO SAY NO TO THE GOOD TO SAY YES TO THE GREAT.

Completing the following exercise will help you avoid the twilight that knows neither victory nor defeat. As you know deep inside—as you have always known—you were born for so much more.

The world needs the mark that only you can make. And it needs you to make it with all your heart.

MY BIG, BRAVE, 90-DAY 'HELL YES!' PLAN

What are my top three priorities I most want to say a big 'Hell Yes!' to over the next 90 days in my work, family, friendships, community, wellbeing or finances? (*Write down specific SMART goals using the format from step 2.*)

Goal 1

Goal 2

Goal 3

How will I feel 3 months from now if I stay on my current path, procrastinate further and let the 'small stuff' keep me from achieving each of the goals above? (*This is about getting real about the cost of inaction.*)

How will I feel 3 months from now if I step into action, daily, and succeed in achieving each of these goals?

For each goal schedule your actions over the next 3 months, e.g. Gym: Mon, Wed and Fri 6–7am.

Who will I enlist from my tribe to make myself accountable?

MY BEST SELF GAME PLAN

First we make our habits and then our habits make us. Living my best life is ultimately about making a habit of finding the good in every situation and feeling good about how I'm 'showing up' for the big game of life. While I can never control all that's going on outside me, I *can* control what's going on inside through the actions I take each day to reconnect with myself, refuel my energy and refocus on what matters most. Here's my game plan for this...

When I wake up each morning, I will set my intention for the day by asking myself: How may I best serve today? To help me remember to do this I will... (*List rituals and activities you will prioritise to stay at your best physically, mentally, emotionally and spiritually.*)

To take care of my body so that I can enjoy the energy and vitality I want, I will... (*Write down what you're committed to with exercise, nutrition, sleep and getting the support you know you will need to stay on track.*)

To ensure I stay focused on what matters most, I will schedule time each week to identify my highest priorities and review them each evening to plan for the day ahead. To ensure this happens I will ... (*schedule time into my calendar ... purchase a weekly/daily planner ... ask someone to hold me accountable*)

Attitude is everything. Every day I will invest time in activities that help me reconnect, recharge and reframe my challenges so I can feel truly grateful, confident, passionate and positive. To ensure this happens I will ... (*write in a gratitude journal ... spend time in nature ... meditate ... pray ... read or listen to uplifting messages ... do something for others ... unplug from my devices ... just 'be' with myself and my family*)

As I step forward to make my unique mark on the world, I choose to live from gratitude, trust my intuition and always remember that I ...

STAY INSPIRED, STAY CONNECTED

Making your own unique mark on the world is a life-long journey. To help you forge your bravest path in your work, relationships, leadership and life, Margie has created a host of inspiring and practical resources she'd love to share with you.

Check them out at www.MargieWarrell.com

While you're there, pick up a copy of Margie's other three bestselling books!

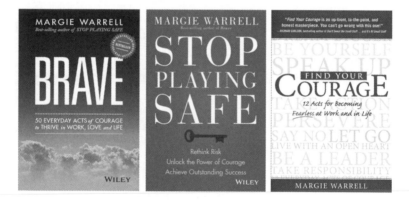

How will you make your mark? Margie would love to hear from you. Stay in touch on social media.

Facebook | Twitter | Instagram | LinkedIn

For speaking, media and all other enquiries email info@margiewarrell.com